Real Estate
CONFRONTS
REALITY

TOM DOOLEY • STEFAN SWANEPOEL • MICHAEL ABELSON

Real Estate
Education Company®
a division of Dearborn Financial Publishing, Inc.

While a great deal of care has been taken to provide accurate and current information, the ideas, suggestions, general principles and conclusions presented in this text are subject to local, state and federal laws and regulations, court cases and any revisions of same. The reader is thus urged to consult legal counsel regarding any points of law—this publication should not be used as a substitute for competent legal advice.

Director, Product Development: Carol L. Luitjens
Senior Acquisitions Editor: Diana Faulhaber
Project Manager: Ronald J. Liszkowski
Art Manager: Lucy Jenkins

Published by Real Estate Education Company,®
a division of Dearborn Financial Publishing, Inc.®

Printed in the United States of America.

98 99 2000 10 9 8 7 6 5 4 3 2 1

ISBN No: 0-7931-2709-2

Library of Congress Cataloging-in-Publication Data

Dooley, Tom, 1932–
    Real estate confronts reality : consumers, computers,
confusion / Tom Dooley, Stefan Swanepoel, Michael A. Abelson :
foreword by Bud Smith.
    p.   cm.
    Includes index.
    ISBN 0–7931–2709–2
    1. Real estate business–United States. 2. Real estate business–
United States–Forecasting.   3. Real estate agents–United States.
I. Swanepoel, Stefan. II. Abelson, Michael A. III. Title.
HD255.D66 1998
333.33'0973–dc21
           97-30580
           CIP

CONTENTS

Contents

FOREWORD

Real Estate, like virtually every area of life, is in a state of continuous change. That rapidity of change is as yet unmeasured but is disconcerting to most everyone in or attached to the business.

Information about the active real estate market as ensconced in the heads of REALTORS® or multiple-listing-service (MLS) systems, seemed for years to be the REALTORS® justification for existence. In fact, that has never been true. In a free market economy, anything that does not add economic value to the transaction ultimately disappears.

The real estate professional adds not just facts and information but knowledge to the transaction—knowledge of the real marketplace, knowledge of what information is necessary for a buyer or seller to make an informed decision and knowledge about all aspects of the transaction. Obviously, the real estate professional has also added marketing, negotiating and empathy to both parties, but the economic value was and is based upon the totality of contribution—not just one or two things.

That is why surveys continue to show a high level of satisfaction with the REALTOR®'s service, even suggesting that almost three-fourths of the public who have used a REALTOR®'s services believe the fee was worth the value of services received.

Technology and the application of that technology to providing information the public wants and needs is a river that cannot, and should not, be dammed up. But rivers of information can drown the recipient—in any field.

For example, how many of us when planning travel can absorb every combination of price, time, connection and service provided that one can obtain on one's own PC, mentally compare all of those alternatives and make the best decision? If I want a four-wheel-drive vehicle, how much information about 15 different products, 43 variations of those products and the hundreds of alternative equipment combinations, prices, etc., can I mentally juggle? You see the point.

The REALTOR® of the future will exist and prosper because he or she can research all that information, as he or she has always done before, but in such a way that he or she can convert that information to knowledge. This knowledge is then passed on to the consumer, enabling the consumer to make a fully informed, best decision for himself.

The people in the industry will no longer deceive themselves into believing they earn their commissions by carefully controlling the information in their MLS books. That was never the primary value added, economically justifying the commission, and never will be in the future.

Real estate decisions are very different from buying stock, travel arrangements or automobiles. In stocks the market is set and known, and one share of IBM is exactly like any other. In travel, destinations are known and price and convenience are the two deciding factors. With automobiles, there is still the need to "try it out," but one Ford Explorer is like any other. I can test drive it in Chicago and buy it (or something identical to it) in Cincinnati.

Not so with property!

Our homes are, indeed, our castles, and no two are exactly alike. Three oak trees in the back yards of two different homes in a city may sound alike but, how they shade the deck and what they look like through the kitchen window are never the same.

People don't just invest in homes—they live in them. They raise families and create memories in them, and thus they have to "fit" perfectly.

While facts (information) are important to have, it is the transformation of these facts into knowledge that allows customers to make one of the most important decisions of their lives.

Let technology destroy the real estate brokerage system of today, and it will be rebuilt tomorrow, not out of greed or business opportunity, but because the public will demand the services it provides.

How real estate companies are structured and operated, how organized real estate exists and what it does, which services the public demands, etc., will continue to change—in fact, even more rapidly over the next five years than over the previous five.

Tom Dooley, Stefan Swanepoel and Michael Abelson have observed and been part of the real estate scene for many years. Theirs is a unique perspective—not one shaped by self-preservation or by self-interest. It behooves everyone connected to housing in any way to read and be challenged by their assumptions, thinking, and planning for the 21st century.

Bud Smith
August 1997

The next few years could mark the end of an era of real estate brokerage as we know it today. Most people say they like progress, but in reality few like change. You see, change is not a spectator sport. You have to participate.

So if you wish to survive, this is your wake-up call. It's time to play.

One of the world's largest industries, the real estate industry, has remained almost unchanged since the 1960s. It is considered by many to be populated by poorly educated practitioners, who preside over a generally unsophisticated and very fragmented industry. Now the industry is at the vortex of three large revolutions:

- the technology revolution,
- the communication revolution, and
- the consumer revolution.

No one can accurately predict what the impact of these revolutions will be, nor can they come up with the total solution for all time, but the time has come for real estate professionals to accept that they can no longer ignore what's happening around them.

The message is clear: Traditional real estate is dead.

The authors of this book hope that the information compiled in this book will help serve as a road map through the coming decade of change.

Stefan Swanepoel
(on behalf of the authors)
August 1997

ACKNOWLEDGMENTS

Many thanks to all the brilliant minds who took precious time out of their already very busy schedules to share with us their knowledge and views of the future. To the many others who have also contributed so freely to the real estate industry—thank you.

Tom, Stefan & Michael

Brian Allen, Co-President, Windermere Realty Services

Bob Arrigoni, Advisor to the President, NRT Inc.

Walter Baczkowski, Jr., Executive Vice, President, San Diego Association of Realtors

Del Bain, President, Del Bain Seminars

Dave Barker, President, Career Education Systems

Chandler Barton, Chairman, NRT Inc.

Robert Becker, President & CEO, NRT Inc.

Bruce Benham, Vice President of Information Technology, RE/MAX International

Dave Beson, President, Dave Beson Seminars

Jerry Bresser, CEO, North America 1 Realty Corp.

Howard Brinton, Owner, Howard Brinton Seminars

Tom Brodnicki, Senior Vice President, Honig Realty

Gary Buda, Vice President of Operations & Systems, Better Homes & Gardens Real Estate Services

Maria Bunting, Co-President, Windermere Realty Services

Peter Burgdorf, President & CEO, ERA Real Estate Network

Stephen Casper, Senior Vice President, West Shell Inc.

Andrew Cimerman, Chairman & CEO, Realty World

Bill Clarkson, President, ERA Golden Hills Brokers

David Cocks, Managing Partner, CompensationMaster

Karen Como, Regional Vice President, ERA Real Estate Network

Richard Cope, Chairman & CEO, The Prudential Florida Realty

Charles Dahlheimer, President, North America Consulting Group

Gary Daniels, Divisional Vice President, Harmon Publishing Company

Richard DeWolfe, Chairman & CEO, The DeWolfe Companies

Richard Didow, Principal & Co-founder, The Personal Marketing Company

Chris Elliot, President, Image Maker Systems

Michael English, Multi Media Consultant

Roy Fair, CEO, Realty Executives Illinois

John Featherston, Publisher, RIS Inc.

Mike Ferry, Chairman & President, The Mike Ferry Organization

Bruce Finland, CEO & President, Member Direct Television

Barney Fletcher, CEO & President, Barney Fletcher Enterprises

Michael Frenkel, Director: Communications, HFS, Inc.

Dennis Galloway, Industry Consultant

Greg Goff, Senior Vice President, Harmon Publishing Company

Dennis Gould, Chief Financial Officer, CompensationMaster

Victor Goulet, Former CEO, ERA Real Estate Network

Jeanne Grainger, Co-President, Windermere Realty Services

Thomas Gregorich, President, Moore Data Management Services

Edward Gresham, Senior Vice President, AmeriNet

Peter Hackes, Production Director, Member Direct Television

Nelson Hansen, Executive Vice President, US Digital

Don Harlan, Partner, Harlan Lyons & Associates

Mac Heavener, President, ERA Services, Inc. (Florida)

Shelia Hensley, President, Executive Relocation Services

Rick Hoffman, President, Coldwell Banker Associates, Realtors (San Diego)

Bradley Inman, President, Inman News Features

Richard Janssen, President, RealSelect, Inc.

Ken Jenny, Industry Analyst

Daryl Jesperson, President, RE/MAX International

Brian June, CEO, US Digital

Kevin Kelleher, President, HFS Mobility Services

Gary Keller, CEO, Keller Williams Real Estate

Mac Kelton, President, ERA Pacesetter Partners

Karun Khanna, Executive Vice President, USWeb System Logic

Robert Kunisch, Vice Chairman, HFS, Inc.

Robert Kyle, Chairman & CEO, Dearborn Publishing Group, Inc.

Fred Levine, President & COO, Harmon Publishing Company

Dave Liniger, Chairman & Co-Founder, RE/MAX International

Gail Liniger, CEO & Co-Founder, RE/MAX International

John Linton, General Counsel, RE/MAX International

Richard Loughlin, Former CEO, Century 21 Real Estate

Gail Lyons, Partner, Harlan, Lyons & Associates

Darryl MacPherson, Senior Vice President, RIS, Inc.

William Malkasian, Executive Vice President, Wisconsin Association of Realtors

Roald Marth, CEO, SUPERSTAR COMPUTING

David Martin, COO, Real Estate Buyer's Agent Council

Ralph Martin, President, Kunkel Realtors

Stephen Martin, President, The Gwent Group

Albert Mayer, Vice President & Independent Consultant, Prudential Real Estate Affiliates

Terrence McDermott, Executive Vice President, NAR

Ron Mechsner, Vice President, HFS

Mark Melton, President, Melton Services, Inc.

Peter Miller, Author: Real Estate Center, America Online Inc.

Robert Moles, President & CEO, Century 21 Real Estate

John Moore, President, Reliance Relocation Services

Laurie Moore-Moore, Co-Editor, REAL Trends

R. Layne Morrill, 1998 President, National Association of REALTORS®

Steve Murray, Co-Editor, REAL Trends

Don Murray, President, American Companies

Pamela O'Connor, President, RELO

Peter Ogden, President, Ogden & Company Realtors

Steven Ozonian, President & CEO, The Prudential Real Estate Affiliates. Inc.

Jack Peckham III, Executive Director, The Real Estate Cyberspace Society

Alex Perriello, President, Coldwell Banker Real Estate

Robert Pittman, President & CEO, AOL Networks, a subsidiary of America Online Inc.

Henry Porterfield, President, Oak Brook Capital

Robert Prince, President & CEO, Homes & Land Magazine

Randy Purcell, President, Top Producer Systems

Richard Rector, Chairman, Realty Executives Inc.

Marcie Roggow, Principal, Creative Learning Systems

Larry Romito, Vice President, The Prudential Real Estate
Affilliates

Jim Rose, CEO, Rose & Krueth Realty Corp.

Allen Sabbag, President, Real Estate Group, Meredith Corporation

Richard Schlott, President, RLS Enterprises

Linda Schwan-Hondros, President, Real Estate, Hondros College

Roger Scommegna, President, The Enterprise Ltd.

Ginger Sherman, Vice President, The Prudential Real Estate
Affiliates

Jim Sherry, President, Interealty

Henry Silverman, Chairman & CEO, HFS, Inc.

George Slusser, Senior Vice President, ERA Real Estate Network

Almon "Bud" Smith, Former Executive Vice President, National
Association of Realtors

Richard Smith, President, Real Estate Division, HFS, Inc.

John Snodgrass, President & Vice Chairman, HFS, Inc.

Gene Stefaniak, President & CEO, Coldwell Banker Equitable-
Stefaniak Realtors

Jacob Stepan, Vice President, HFS, Inc.

Rob Stockus, Industry Consultant

Donald Streeter, Industry Consultant

Becky Swann, President, International Real Estate Digest

John Tuccillo, Consulting Economist to NAR

Hugo "Skip" Weber, President, Polley & Associates

John Wendorff, Chairman, The Personal Marketing Company

Dave Westfall, Executive Vice President, RE/MAX International

Stewart Wilson, Vice President, AON

Stuart Wolff, CEO, RealSelect Inc.

CHAPTER 1

Crazed, Confused or Cause for Celebration?

"If you're not ready to embrace massive change in our industry, then prepare, dinosaur, for your march to the tar pits."

Ken Jenny, Industry Analyst

"Get rid of bricks and sticks, get rid of overhead—it's time to change."

Bob Pittman, former CEO of Century 21

What do you think of when you hear the word *change?* A new century, one world economy, burgeoning new technology? The fact that the new millennium is upon us is really insignificant. Looking back with hindsight we will probably see that the two largest changes in our industry where the influence of consumerism and the way technology has changed and will continue to change our entire world.

Most people acknowledge that things are changing but don't really grasp the long-term impact of these changes. Perhaps only a small percentage cares enough to try and understand the meaning and ramifications of what is happening. The reality is, however, the unchallenged existence that real estate has enjoyed for decades will not go unchallenged any longer.

This time, the change in the real estate industry is coming; it is not just another rumor or passing fad. This time, it

1

is for real. It is serious. It is potentially so extensive that it will affect everyone in the real estate industry—brokerages, mortgage lenders, title companies, as well as the numerous other participants in the home-buying and home-selling transaction.

Who is driving the change? you might ask. The consumer. Consumers themselves have changed dramatically during the last few years, and their demands on the industry are increasingly requiring different solutions and activities. Buying a home and applying for a mortgage has become a process—a painful, time-consuming process. It shouldn't be a process; it should be an event. Pleasant, quick and easy.

The reality of this change is being received with mixed emotion by the real estate industry. Known for the tardiness in accepting change, real estate practitioners will have to realize that this time they have no choice, because if they don't change, the majority of them will be employed elsewhere in the not-too-distant future. Although the future is unpredictable at best, what is clear is that it will be different, very different within a couple of years.

WHY THE CURRENT STATUS REQUIRES CHANGING

Currently, there are some one million agents in the United States. Some 720,000 of them are members of the National Association of REALTORS® (NAR) (Refer to Chapter 2—"NAR: Growing, Going or Gone?"—for more details.) and are estimated to be the number of full-timer real estate practitioners. Allen Sabbag, president of Merediths Real Estate, who believes that the number of practitioners earning their main source of income from real estate could actually be as low as 350,000.

According to NAR statistics, the number of REALTORS® has been declining steadily over the last decade until last year. Virtually everyone you speak to is predicting that the

FIGURE 1.1 Number of Real Estate Professionals

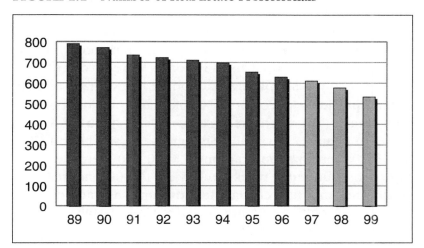

decline will continue into the early portion of the next century. Depending on who you favor, the number could end up anywhere between 100,000 and 500,000 (see Figure 1.1). John Tucillo, consulting Economist to NAR, has frequently been quoted as saying that 50 percent of the real estate practitioners in five years are not in the industry today. If we accept the prediction that the number of real estate practitioners will probably halve in the next five to ten years, then that will equate to some 5,000 real estate practitioners leaving the industry every month for the next five years.

Secondly, the real estate industry is fragmented, entrepreneurial and volatile. True industry standards are hard to define and in many instances just don't exist. Rules are difficult to enforce, and industrywide consistency is almost completely absent. The total structure of the home-buying and home-selling process is further more largely built on the compilation of various industries, such as the real estate practitioners, the appraisers, the mortgage originators and lenders and the title companies. They all thrive off of one another, mainly as a result of the inefficiencies of the process, duplicating the same information and saturating the home-buying process.

Bradley Inmar, founder of Inmar News, recently bought a house in San Francisco, and shares the experience by noting that 47 different people and 110 forms were involved.

"It is really a simple transaction," says Richard Schlott, former president of Schlott REALTORS® and president of ERA Real Estate, "yet we make it so complex." "You know it is going to change," says John Snodgrass, president and COO of HFS "when someone can buy a $150,000 Mercedes in an afternoon but needs weeks to buy a $150,000 house." And if service can affect change, it is dynamic newcomer mega company. (Refer to Chapter 3—"HFS: Cash! Catalyst!? Committed!?"—for more detail.)

Thirdly, the foundation on which the real estate transaction was built, the listing data, has until now been carefully controlled by the real estate practitioners. In the past, the NAR, through the numerous local MLS systems, created a power base and made the real estate practitioner the central component to the transaction. That control over the data has allowed prices to be almost fixed and has kept change back. "They are about to lose that control," says Schlott. "Soon the consumer will be able to go to many different sources of information," he adds.

The era of unlimited access to information is now upon us, and "the data the industry covered so long now has no value anymore," says Jim Sherry, president of Interealty, the nation's largest MLS. According to Sherry, the industry is littered with proprietary systems, a legacy of the growth of the MLS systems over three decades. Today the Internet is creating a new open standard, easy—inexpensive and unlimited access to data, 24 hours a day, 7 days a week, from anywhere. So, if information is power, then access by the consumer to more information will transfer the power to the consumer.

Fourth, and by no means last, is the fact that numerous real estate related and nonrelated companies are investigating the industry and questioning the current inefficiencies. As a matter of fact, most industry experts are certain that the drivers that will change the real estate industry will not be coming from within, but from the outside. Many speculate that the mortgage banks have the strongest desire to control the point of sale in the home-buying process.

Ken Jenny, an independent real estate analyst, says that one of the biggest question being asked is, "How does one prepare for these numerous changes that seem to be inevitable?" According to Jenny, the real estate industry is made up of some of the most entrepreneurial people in all of business today. It is therefore necessary for the industry to honestly answer some tough questions. Can real estate companies like RE/MAX, The Realty Alliance and the large players (refer to Chapter 4—"Chasing Number 1"—for more details) still add value to the transaction? Value that justifies a payment of 6 percent to 7 percent of the price of the transaction?

Will there come a time when consumers no longer need the services of a traditional real estate practitioner?

It is generally accepted that the real estate practitioner does contribute to the transaction, in many cases substantially; however, to what extent is he or she needed and to what extent should he or she be remunerated remains to be seen. We also know that the number of real estate agents is coming down and the number of transactions is fairly constant, so that at least should mean more money left for those real estate practitioners remaining. So there will be less for less, and if you're one of the ones surviving, it might mean more for you. If you're one of the ones surviving, that is.

Commissions of real estate practitioners have been a controversial point for a long time. According to John Moore, president of Genesis Relocation Services commissions are going down all over the country. He also expects that "consumers will negotiate commissions down even further." The industry generates approximately $33 billion of commissions every year, yet when evaluating the gross income of real estate practitioners, one finds that only one in four earns more than $50,000 a year. Almost half earn less than $25,000 a year. (Refer to Chapter 8—"Are Brokers and Agents Overpaid?"—for details.)

Allen Sabbag President, Real Estate Group, Meredith Corporation, agrees that commissions will go down but says that "the decline will be gradual until more savvy consumers will ultimately effect an evolutionary change in the way real estate salespeople are remunerated."

The general consensus is that consumers are not trying to eliminate the real estate practitioner. But we do know that the consumer people is changing rapidly (Refer to Chapter 5—"Demographics: Your Secret Weapon!"—for more details), want value, and if the real estate industry gives it to them that's great. If the industry doesn't give them what they want, they will vote with their feet and go elsewhere.

Numerous components of the transactions are changing; for example, it is clear that the listing side of the transaction is under siege. Sellers will in the future need real estate practitioners less than they need them today. So this portion of the pie will also shrink. Maybe the industry is actually to blame for this decline, and not the consumer or technology. As a result of the exclusive control REALTORS® enjoyed over listings in the past, the industry ignored the importance of this component of the transaction and subsequently did a poor job of selling their value to the listing side of the transaction. And when consumers no longer believe someone is adding value, they go around him or her. We all like to buy wholesale, getting a good price. It's simple: the person with the best deal wins. "The consumers' most noteworthy impact will probably be in the area of pricing, where we will see radical change in the standard six to seven percent commission," says Jenny.

So what is the solution to the changing needs of the consumer? Simple. Give him value. Save him time. Make the process easy and pleasant. Linda Hondross, a leading real estate trainer, believes that consumers of the future will not want to come down to your office to find out what is going on. They will want to "shop for real estate in their jammies," she says. Moore agrees with the statement as far as preselection but adds that "they still are going to want to do some tire kicking before they buy." The solution is, of course, to give consumers a fee-based service which allows them to select the services they need directly from the convenience of their homes. Let them pay only for what they use, and you will have a good chance of keeping them. (Refer for more details to Chapter 6—"Can Consumers Control the Inside Track?"—and Chapter 7—"Agents: A Profession in Question.")

TECHNOLOGY FLOODGATES OPEN

The personal computer (PC) was the first watershed event that introduced the dramatic change that we're seeing. For the first time, the PC brought low-cost, high-speed processing down to a desktop level for the average user. The second technology that came shortly after the PC was the use of graphical interfaces, which allowed nonprogrammers and nontechnicians to easily use a PC. The third advent was the low cost for memory and for storage. (*Memory* is the temporary device that keeps instructions and data in the machine's processor while it is turned on. *Storage* is the long-term device that keeps the information on a hard drive when the computer is turned off.) The fourth advent has been the faster and faster processors. The last bastion or real impediment to universal microcomputing fell in approximately 1994 with the advent of the World Wide Web. This is leading to gigantic networks of unprecedented capacity, reducing scale economies and putting more value on efficiency and individual creativity.

The first major technological event was when programming changed linear sequential assembly line code, called

TABLE 1.1 Growth of Technology Power

Intel Chip	Date	Initial Cost	Transistors	Initial Mips*
4004	11/71	$ 200	2,300	0.06
8008	4/72	300	3,500	0.06
8080	4/74	300	6,000	0.06
8086	6/78	360	29,000	0.3
8088	6/79	360	29,000	0.3
i286	2/82	360	134,000	0.9
i386	10/85	299	275,000	5.0
i486	4/89	950	1,200,000	20.0
Pentium	3/93	878	3,100,000	100.0
Pentium Pro	3/95	974	5,500,000	300.0
786†	1997	1,000	8,000,000	500.0
886†	2000	1,000	15,000,000	1,000.0

*MIPS = Million instructions per second
†Industry estimates

Sources: Kleiner, Perkins, Caulfield & Byers; Intel Corp., Dataquest Inc.

procedural code. This was a single-tasking exercise, meaning the computer could only do one thing at a time. Today's computers are nonsequentially programmed, with object-oriented, or neuro-networks or inference engines. Programmed graphically, they can do many, many things, all at once. This allows computers that, with neuro-network's inference engines to emulate the human mind.

One fascinating observation in technology has been referred to as Moore's Law. This theory says that technology—particularly information processing power—doubles every 18 months. This seems to have been true for the last 25 years and is expected to continue for at least the next 10 years (see Table 1.1).

The overall impact over time is huge. For example, in 1971 the first microprocessor executed 60,000 instructions per second while a processor in the year 2000 is expected to process one billion transactions per second. So where does all this growth end? Humans have always favored the theory that we are above all else in this world and the supreme beings in this environment called our world. Humans believed they were the only ones in the universe. Galileo challenged that. Then humans believed they were created unique. Darwin questioned that. Then humans believed only they had the ability to reason.

And now reason, considered by many to be the final frontier, has been challenged. Chess, considered by some as the ultimate game in human intelligence, has become the measuring stick of that ability. Could a computer created by human beings, actually eclipse man at his own game? For decades the answer has been an unequivocal no. On May 11, 1997, the ultimate battle between man and machine, considered the final stance of humanity against the creeping tide of technological superiority, took place. The impossible happened. An IBM customized RS/6000 supercomputer, called Deep Blue, became the first-ever piece of technology to defeat the reigning world chess champion. With the ability to evaluate 200 million alternatives per second, Deep Blue proved that artificial intelligence need not attempt to emulate the brain in order to surpass it.

Can reason be reproduced? Is this the beginning of artificial intelligence?

Does it matter? No, not really. The message is, however, clear. You need to change your thinking.

Since 1994 the pace has become so fast that "it's nearly impossible to stay abreast of all the changes affecting real estate" according to John Featherston, publisher of *National Real Estate and Relocation* magazine. So can real estate practitioners survive? Sure, but real estate practitioners will have to "get away from their independent contractor mentality," says Robert Kyle, president of Dearborn Publishing Group, the nation's largest publisher of real

TABLE 1.2 Top Five Technology Trends for the Year 2001

1. The information explosion and the consumer's access to real estate information
2. The impact of technology on the reengineering of the way real estate business will be conducted
3. Growth of the Internet and broader use in real estate
4. The rearranging of services offered by real estate agents as a result of technology
5. The decline in the number of real estate agents as a result of technology

Source: US Digital Research, Summer 1997

estate books. The industry has an uneven product of people coming into the industry, according to Kyle, and this complicates creating standardized systems in the industry. Technology is now going to change that. Consider technology an ongoing consumption tool, and like stationery, you have to buy new supplies regularly. Leading industry technology trainer Roald Marth says, "Feed your body food and your brain technology." (Refer to Chapter 9—"Is Tech the Ticket to Ride?"—for more details.)

Five key technology trends are expected to form the basis for the real estate model for the 21st century (see Table 1.2).

"The real estate industry has always been paranoid about technology," says Inmar. The solution, of course, is not to be scared of technology or any other changes, but to find more effective ways to sell real estate with all the new tools—database direct marketing, localized shopping publications, interactive voice marketing and messaging telephone systems and worldwide on-line marketing.

Can you do it?

Sure.

Will you?

Probably not.

Will someone else?

Yes.

When?

Soon.

If the real estate industry does not find ways to provide complete services and information, the market will find ways of doing without them. There is a growing pull by the consumer to bundle the services of the home-buying transaction together, not necessarily under one roof, but as one seamless transaction. Consumers might not get one-stop real estate shopping today, but they will get it, and soon. That's what they have come to expect in most other walks of life and business. One-stop shopping (Refer to Chapter 10—"One Step Shopping"—for more details.) is already visible in many other industries and real estate is definitely now on the next list. You don't think so? Unfortunately, no reason you give will make a difference. Consumers don't really care what real estate practitioners think or want. It's what they think and want. And they want convenience. And they want one-stop shopping.

Be warned; the consumers get what they want, and they want one-stop shopping. Great if you're the shop—a problem if you're not.

CHAPTER 2

NAR: Growing, Going or Gone?

"Of course the decline or possible demise of NAR is not an absolute given because it may be visionary enough and able to get out of its own way. But I doubt it! I hope they are but sometimes I wonder."

Brian June, U.S. Digital Corporation

Is the National Association of REALTORS® (NAR) in danger of becoming extinct, or obsolete, or irrelevant?

Will technology change the landscape of the real estate business so rapidly as to leave the NAR in its wake, washing it ashore as a historic fossil?

Will the shift from the entrepreneurial ownership that characterized the real estate industry throughout most of its history to the current era of corporate "Wall Street–type" ownership present the NAR with challenges it is unable to master?

Or will the real estate brokerage industry itself yield its long-standing position as the hub of the wheel for property transactions to other contenders, such as mortgage lenders, and as a result downgrade its trade association to the level of a minimal fringe organization?

Given such sets of potential circumstances it is easy—and almost logical—to sound the death knell on the NAR.

Many are the doomsayers who are more than willing—perhaps even anxious—to write finis over the 90-year old association. At conferences where leading real estate practitioners gather to discuss the future of their industry, negative attitudes toward the NAR are expressed:

"We certainly would not want to change shoes with the NAR, not with all its problems and criticisms."

"Even when it comes to arbitration cases, no major broker pays any attention to the NAR or to the local board."

"Everything they do, they screw up—except the regular collection of dues from members."

"To think that the NAR serves any purpose to the big broker other than legislative is foolish."

But before we summarily declare the organization destined for extinction, let us not fail to thoroughly examine its actual current state of health as well as its past history of "near death" struggles with what, in their time, were often diagnosed as "life-threatening" situations for the NAR.

Over the course of its long history, the National Association of REALTORS® has been confronted with a variety of severe challenges. Although some of these challenges were considered virtually insurmountable, the NAR has always managed to either overcome, co-op or adapt to such occasions:

- The conversion from "vest pocket" listings to Realtor-to-Realtor cooperation
- The extension of Realtor-to-Realtor cooperation through the creation and development of multiple listing services (MLSs)
- The shift from "open" to "exclusive" listings
- The conversion from racial exclusion in membership and, often, in clientele to "open housing" and "affirmative action"

- The onset of the "100 percent commission concept" and the resulting major shift in commission division structures and brokerage profitability
- The elimination of "fixed," or even "recommended," rates of commission and replacement with totally free and negotiated market concepts
- The conversion from a political policy that was essentially reactionary and single-party focused to one that is proactive on behalf of real estate interests and opportunistic in terms of candidate support
- The absorption of salespersons into REALTOR® classification and NAR membership
- The spinoff of such staunch members of the NAR family as the American Institute of Real Estate Appraisers and the International Federation
- The court requirement that MLSs must be open and available to licensees other than REALTORS®
- The demand for and adoption of the "Board of Choice" concept
- The recent debacle of the REALTORS® Information Network (RIN)

There were rumors of the NAR's pending demise in connection with many, if not all, of these traumatic shifts in the status quo.

They have all proven to be quite inaccurate.

So in all likelihood are today's forecasts of imminent demise or dissolution because of pent-up discontent among many members, especially those commanding large market share.

BEST BET? THE NAR STAYS, BUT WITH CHANGES

Many veteran knowledgeable industry observers are betting that the NAR will survive and prosper. And, as in the past, it will emerge from threatening situations with somewhat different characteristics of structure and operation than it had before it confronted the challenges.

THE WISCONSIN REALTOR® ASSOCIATION MODEL

In terms of governance and organizational structure, the model for the NAR's future may already be in existence, in the Wisconsin REALTOR® Association (WRA), which in 1997 adopted a totally new format for representation and decision making within the organization. Wisconsin revamped its "power structure" by reducing membership in its directorate from a one-time high of 200 to just 32 and by restructuring the constituent groups represented on the board of directors as well as totally remodeling the procedure for election and/or appointment to the body.

As implemented for the first time in an election process concluded in June 1997, the Wisconsin State directorate is comprised of the following categories of members:

1. One representative from each of the three largest firms in the state. These individuals must be either owners or managers of a firm. For purposes of tabulation in this category, each franchised office is counted as one individual firm. The terms of these representatives are one year each. Should one of the largest companies decline to serve, a representative of the next largest company would be chosen as a replacement.

2. One representative from the largest firm headquartered in each of seven geographic regions into which the state has been divided. These too will serve one-year terms. Those firms represented by virtue of being one of the three largest in the state (as stated in number 1, above) are not eligible for additional representation under the regional category.

3. Eleven representatives elected by the total membership of the association (about 11,000 eligible voters).
   A form of population representation will apply in
   this category in that there will be one director chosen for each 1,200 members in a region. (Thus, a
   region with 1,250 members would be entitled to one
   director, while a region with 3,750 members would
   get three representatives.) Persons elected under this
   category shall serve three-year terms but they were
   to be staggered during the first three years. Any
   REALTOR® member of WRA is eligible for inclusion on
   this ballot, simply by being nominated either by himself or herself or by someone else. Only REALTORS®
   who have been members of the board for at least
   three years are eligible to vote and may cast votes
   only for candidates in the region in which they primarily operate. In order to be elected under this category, a person must receive at least 33 percent of the
   vote cast. In the absence of a 33 percent plurality for
   the number of posts to be filled in a specific region,
   there will be a runoff election.
4. Five members of the association's executive committee (the president, president-elect, treasurer and two
   vice presidents) who shall have automatic ex post
   facto inclusion on the board. Each shall serve a one-
   year term.
5. Three past presidents of the association who will be
   selected by the past presidents' council for one-year
   terms.
6. Three "outside directors" appointed by the executive
   committee, upon recommendation by the executive
   vice president. These persons are expected to be
   chosen from organizations that have a commonality
   or mutuality of interest with the real estate profession but these individuals will not hold a real estate
   license.

Any of the directors may be reelected or reappointed to their posts but none may serve more than four consecutive terms.

Balloting for elective spots shall be by mail beginning in mid-May and ending approximately three weeks later.

Under the new arrangement, members of the executive committee will continue to be elected by the board of directors.

One major objective accomplished by the Wisconsin structure is to, in effect, force the involvement of leaders of major firms in the governance process. By allotting automatic slots for large firms, the arrangement answers the criticism that organized real estate is not attentive to its major practitioners, being run instead by entrepreneurs of smaller firms who have either the time or interest or both to become active in organizational politics. At the same time, there is forced participation of the megabrokerage firms, and not just by some minor functionary assigned the task but rather only by the owner/proprietor or designated managing broker.

According to William E. Malkasian, executive vice president of the Wisconsin Association, now that the new structure is in place, the board of directors will probably meet no more than three times per year. Unlike previous arrangements, these meetings shall not be conducted in conjunction with various gatherings of the association membership. There will continue to be committees and/or advisory groups appointed by the board to undertake and oversee various projects. These will report to the board when they have some recommendation that requires a board decision.

"In essence," Malkasian says, "what we are doing is eliminating all purely administrative meetings and concentrating instead on board attention to policy matters. In addition." he notes, "we have reduced the function of the Wisconsin State Association to a concentration on those things that are its core competencies. Principally, these are public policy matters in the fields of legislative activity and license law matters."

"The association will continue to have a strong presence in member education," Malkasian adds, "but aside from that we will be withdrawing from the board services arena, leaving functions there either to local and regional associations or to the National Association of REALTORS®."

Under the new structure, Malkasian foresees the day when organized real estate in Wisconsin will consist of the state association and "probably eight to ten strong regional associations." "And, of course," he states, "we all will continue to be members of the NAR."

In a practical sense, Malkasian believes that representation on association committees and special task forces will be balanced among the various regions.

Necessity may well have been the mother of invention in the Badger State. For the past couple of years, prominent REALTORS® there have been seriously questioning the existing framework of organized real estate. Many alleged that there was serious duplication of effort and duplication (and often triplication) of expenses to carry out such efforts. Some proposed a solution to the problem by suggesting the elimination of the State Association of REALTORS® and reliance solely on local boards. Others said terminate the local boards and filter any unduplicated work to the state association. Some even proposed a "stand-alone" situation for each level of the current tripart Realtor organization, establishing membership in the local, state and national associations as a voluntary—and totally independent—choice on the part of practitioners. Thus, using a model employed by the bar associations and the chambers of commerce, a licensee could belong to one, two or three of the REALTOR® organizations but need not belong to one in order to have membership in another.

Whether the new Wisconsin State Association governance structure will satisfy those who favor somewhat harsher alterations in the status quo remains to be seen.

Malkasian freely admits, "We have yet to see how all of this will work, but we are extremely optimistic that it will be successful, largely because it is the result of a tremendous amount of input from REALTORS® from throughout the state."

"Have no doubt about it," he clarifies. "This system is in place because of the diligence and hard work of hundreds of REALTORS® who had input to the process. You also must realize that a substantial number of association leaders voted themselves out of office in order to initiate the new system."

Gene Stefaniak, president of Milwaukee's Coldwell Banker Equitable–Stefaniak REALTORS®, agrees totally, after serving on the committee that assisted the board leadership in fashioning the new structure. "The committee set out to find a means of empowering the people who are truly active in the business while at the same time not overlooking the input of all members. I think we accomplished our task but only after a number of compromises and a lot of consultation with REALTORS® from all parts of the state and from all segments of the industry." One of the compromises allows a "designated managing broker" to serve on the directorate, filling one of the automatic large brokerage posts. "Originally we were going to confine it to the broker/ owner, but there was a lot of sentiment that many owners had too many obligations to devote the needed attention to association matters on a regular basis."

On another point, however, the drafters of the new model were steadfast. There will not be any representation on the directorate by individuals holding sales associate or affiliate membership in the state association. "For some time," Malkasian explains, "it has been apparent that the 'customer' of the state association is the broker/owner and/ or his or her corporate entity. That's who we are serving, and that's who will be serving on the board." Malkasian adds that most of the services and benefits available to and needed by sales associates tend to be provided by local boards and associations and by the NAR or one of its affiliate bodies.

SOME STEPS ARE BEING TAKEN BY THE NAR

While it remains questionable whether the NAR will ever adopt a governance equivalent to Wisconsin's, there is ample evidence that some people in positions of leadership in the National Association of REALTORS® have ideas for a structure somewhat akin to the Badger State's. And some initial steps have already been taken.

At its spring 1996 meetings, the NAR Leadership Team proposed a series of alterations that it saw as "streamlining" the group's method of representation and operation. Among the proposals were

- automatic inclusion of representatives of leading franchise groups and regional megabrokers on the board of directors;
- reduction in the size of the board and shortening in the term of members;
- eventual elimination of at least one of the NAR's annual general membership meetings; and
- elimination of the delegate body (a superstructural gathering of board and state association presidents and others who have final say on any matter pertaining to a change in the association's bylaws.)

Neither the board of directors, then numbering 710, nor the more than 2,000 member delegate body of the NAR saw things exactly the same way as those proposing the changes. The directors supported the notion of dissolving the delegate body but balked at changes to its own composition. The delegate body steadfastly refused to vote itself out of existence.

But, the thumbs-down response did not bury the idea of reorganization. At its May 1997 meetings, the NAR's Leadership Team again proposed a series of changes in the governance structure of the organization designed to accomplish the twofold goal of adding automatic representation for major industry participants on the directorate and streamlining the entire membership by reducing certain other representations. At that meeting, the Leadership Team got about half of what it was seeking from the board of directors. After an extensive floor debate about the most appropriate means to modernize its governance process, the NAR directors voted to approach a "streamlining" process, not by reducing but rather by expanding the number of persons on the board—by 130 delegates—raising the total assemblage to a membership of 840. Essentially, the move opens slots on the board automatically to representatives from the 75 largest companies in the NAR, as measured by the number of sales agents with the firm, as well as to national franchise organizations having at least 150 franchisees and local associations (boards) of REALTORS® having at least 3,000 members. Beyond this expansion, the composition and representation on the directorate would remain as is. To be effective, the change must be approved by the entire NAR delegate body. The additions to the directorate are expected to receive a thumbs-up vote of that large body at the association's national convention in November 1997. At that time, there may be another effort at reducing the overall membership on the board. Any such new approach is not be expected to contain a provision for the assembly to vote itself out of existence.

Whatever the ultimate organizational structure, some of the functions in which NAR will continue to be involved are fairly obvious. Among them are:

- political action in behalf of causes and candidates advantageous to the real estate profession and the particular interests of NAR members;

- custodian, protector and disseminator of the REAL-TOR®'s Code of Ethics, and amendments thereto and interpretations thereof;
- generic and specific public relations activities designed to promote and advance the cause of private ownership of property and the use of REALTORS® in transactions involving same;
- accumulation, analysis and distribution of economic and statistical data pertaining to real estate (which ties in with effective public relations); and
- legal interpretation and assistance to individual members and constituent boards and state associations.

The style and manner in which the NAR conducts such activities may change dramatically. For example, a growing number of directors and other key personnel in the association are suggesting a decision-making process that would replace the current time-consuming voting operation. In the past, an idea presented at one of the NAR's three annual meetings may have had to wait for two or three additional meetings (a year or more) before it reached the stage (if it ever did) where it could be voted upon by the directorate. Instead of this process, a procedure is being suggested to inform members of proposals, solicit and receive their input and then vote—all through the use of e-mail. It may soon be that a prerequisite for nomination to the NAR directorate will be the ability to communicate via e-mail or some other form of Internet-type communications. As a step toward such goals, 1998 will be the last year in which NAR will have three regularly scheduled meetings of its governing councils. Subsequently, the number will be two, with a previously traditional midwinter gathering eliminated.

There are also a number of potential areas of activity that NAR is most likely to avoid:

- Educational offerings (reserved for institutes, local boards, state associations and private purveyors)

- Sales of promotional products and/or office-related materials
- Any commercial venture in competition with free-enterprise activities, especially if those activities are undertaken by members
- Publications requiring financial subsidization beyond subscription revenue and/or advertising

There is also a collection of "maybes" that could or could not fall within the province of a well-run trade or professional association such as the NAR:

- Trade shows and exhibits (Terrence P. "Terry" McDermott, NAR executive vice president as of September 1, 1997, has a record from his previous post as EO of the American Institute of Architects for "outsourcing" major association activities such as conventions and meetings.)
- Economic research and financial analysis on a macro basis
- Extensive industry public relations and publicity
- Research and development

Interconnected with decisions regarding NAR functions and activities is the matter of staffing. Many critics of the National Association of REALTORS® claim that it (and the rest of organized real estate) is overstaffed and, in effect, employs a cadre of bureaucrats who consistently find new activities for the association in order to retain and advance their own professional ambitions.

SMITH ACTUALLY MADE REMARKABLE CHANGES

Such criticism seems totally inconsistent with the facts at the NAR, at least as it was run from 1991 to 1997 under the direction of then Executive Vice President Dr. Almon R. "Bud" Smith. From the beginning of his tenure, Smith flattened the management structure of the NAR, steadily reducing the number of upper-level and middle-level executives while following the principle of subsidiarity in directing decision-making activities to the lowest possible level. Smith continually empowered the NAR personnel with large measures of authority and accountability and, in so doing, was able to establish a ratio of activities to personnel considerably lower than when he came into office. To be exact, the number of NAR employees shrunk from 540 when Smith assumed the executive vice presidency to 375— a 31 percent reduction—at his retirement at the end of August 31, 1997.

To be sure, some of the reductions were attributable to the NAR's evacuation from a number of enterprises no longer deemed to be a part of the core competence of the association. In the six years of Smith's administration, the NAR altered its positions in such areas as product development and sales, public relations, and headquarters building management and reduced substantially its activities in education, association management (for small boards), communications, conferences and specialized divisions. Its role in these areas shifted from that of a provider to that of an advisor or facilitator.

Yet perceptions persist on the part of many members that the NAR is "overstaffed" and "underachieving." One wonders if some of these observers are not confusing the NAR proper with the totality of the National Association of REALTORS® and its aggregate of eight institutes, societies and councils, each of which has a staff of its own. True, each of the affiliate groups also has a mission dedicated to servicing the pronounced needs or wants of a given niche in the real estate community. And each is funded independently, and voluntarily, by the members of that niche.

Recent subtleties seem to indicate that, perhaps to overcome the perception of being "top-heavy," the NAR is distancing itself somewhat from its institutes, societies and councils.

The total number of these affiliated groups is at its lowest level in several decades, after such groups as the American Institute of Real Estate Appraisers (AIREA) and the International Federation (FIABCI) spun off into independent organizations. In addition, the NAR has granted the affiliates a growing amount of autonomy. For example, it was recently determined that there is no longer a requirement nor a necessity for the affiliates to have their meetings held either at the same time or in the same locale as the NAR meetings. In its latest foray into a specialized field, when it acquired the Real Estate Buyer's Agent Council (REBAC) in late 1996, the NAR structured the acquisition as a wholly owned but separate corporation rather than place it under the institute framework.

THE REALTORS® INFORMATION NETWORK (RIN)—AN EXPENSIVE FLOP

If NAR ever needed a rationale for withdrawing from "nontraditional" association activities and concentrating on its "main mission," its ill-fated excursion into the development and operation of the REALTORS® Information Network (RIN) provided such—with emphasis!

In theory, at least at the time of the RIN's creation, the idea of a REALTOR® controlled, consumer accessible Internet site, containing a photo and descriptive inventory of available REALTOR® listings from coast to coast, made some sense. The case for it was made vigorously by William Chee, then president of NAR and later chairman of the RIN Board of Directors. He warned that if the NAR did not get involved in such an activity, other non-REALTOR® entities would do so, capturing control of consumers and, ultimately, of the whole real estate industry. Or, as Chee so eloquently expressed it, "The hungry lions are about to come over the mountain to steal the food from the Chihuahuas, leaving the latter with only bones, if anything."

But NAR involvement with the Internet and the world of cyberspace needed more than eloquence—and more than a hastily conceived and inadequately controlled REALTORS® Information Network could provide.

Establishing the RIN cost NAR a very substantial amount of money, an actual drain of nearly $16 million from the NAR treasury.

Quite correctly, many REALTORS® saw the venture as a highly speculative one—financed entirely by their dues dollars.

Their cause for concern may have been muted if the RIN had met with success.

In reality, it was a colossal flop. A multimillion dollar flop!

From its very beginning, smooth "spin-doctoring" by top executives and public relations–type promises of greatness attempted to vest the RIN with a halo presence. But in reality, RIN's problems were substantial at its beginning and intensified steadily throughout its relatively brief existence. The following are among those most often vocalized by its opponents and latter-day critics:

- Use of the wrong systems and standards
- Insistence on what, in effect, was an "Intranet" system when the universe of cyberspace enthusiasts was hooked on an Internet system
- A marketing and promotional campaign that greatly outpaced the RIN's ability to produce what it promised
- Questionable, if not totally improper, financial and fiscal controls
- Ineptitude and nonaccountability of top management
- Lack of proper oversight by the RIN's Board of Directors and, ultimately, the NAR's leadership.
- Failure to recognize that while the potentially competitive "lions" found in the lairs of non–real estate firms

might be considering coming over the hill, progressive companies in the real estate field, generally regarded as stalwarts of the NAR, were proceeding at their own rapid pace to use the Internet for many of the same functions envisioned by the NAR but were doing so by directing their own resources to systems that would give them competitive advantages over their fellow REALTORS®. In other words, they were seeking to unlevel the playing field in their favor at the same time that the RIN (and the NAR) were committed to leveling that field.

Less than two years after its launching fanfare, the RIN reached its demise amid charges of gross ineptitude and, by some, unethical if not illegal conduct by its CEO.

Suddenly, critics and opponents of the National Association of REALTORS® had three additional powerful arguments to use against it:

1. The NAR was entering fields in which it was a direct competitor of many of its members, including some of the most substantial ones.
2. It was using the funds (i.e., dues dollars) of the very members with whom it was competing to finance such adventures.
3. It was "wasting" the money in ill-conceived and failed efforts.

Few of the critics of the NAR were placated by the fact that the organization's leadership undertook a "rescue what you can" mission after the RIN's demise and wound up structuring a new entity—RealSelect—in which it has only a 15 percent interest but no further investment of funds. RealSelect offers the possibility of ultimate recovery of the RIN losses and maybe even net profit through participation in any dividends that it may generate in the future.

Instead, many brokerages, especially the larger firms and franchise organizations, have proceeded with dispatch to develop, extend and upgrade their own presences on the Internet. Some give homage to the NAR and RealSelect by interlinking their Web sites to RealSelect and vice versa. Others go strictly the independent route, realizing that a consumer who exercises a "hit" on their own site is, for the moment, at least, a captive customer. Those customers who access RealSelect have an array of inventory possibilities, including all competitors' listings—hardly the "unleveled playing field" desired by a highly competitive company. While RealSelect seems to be succeeding, the number of independent company and individual sites has continually expanded.

NO GENERAL UPRISING AGAINST NAR

While there has been and continues to be a rather extensive vocalization of dissatisfaction with the NAR, thus far there has been nothing resembling a "general uprising."

Instead, there are outward expressions of support for the association, provided it avoids extraneous activities and "represents the best interests of the total real estate community." But at the same time, if there are realms of activity in which the NAR is perceived as "competing with" or "working contrary to" their interests, individual REALTORS® firms or groups will combat the association's efforts with the same diligence and skill that they would apply against any other competitor.

Some caution that NAR could collapse of its own momentum—or lack thereof. One such critic is Brian June, CEO of US Digital. As June sees it, the widening of the availability of MLS to non-REALTORS®, ramifications of the board of choice situation, consumer access to the World Wide Web, and the fact that, increasingly, the association will see a strong decline in revenue give reason to wonder about NAR's staying power. He says that if NAR is not able to get out of its

own way the demise of the National Association of REAL-
TORS® could be a possibility. He hedges this bet, but only
moderately, stating, "Of course the elimination of the NAR
and state and local boards, is not an absolute given because
the NAR and some of the stronger state boards may be
visionary enough and able to get out of their own way and
take measures to prevent these occurrences. But I doubt it!"

CHALLENGES THERE MAY WELL BE . . .

In the future, such intensity of opposition to NAR may be
mitigated by the profession collectively, focusing its concern and competitive energy against a "common threat"—a
new major rival, external to the industry, that threatens to
disturb the "status quo" far more than any actions of the
NAR.

When previous NAR difficulties and survivals (or, in
some cases, triumphs) are analyzed closely, it is apparent
that many of the threats were posed by rivals and entities
outside the industry. Faced with a confrontation from without, NAR members typically rallied together, even though
they may not have agreed with every NAR policy and procedure.

So too might it be in the future. Major brokerage firms
and organizations that are far less than totally satisfied with
the state of affairs in the NAR may, nonetheless, rally solidly
behind it if a major external challenger attacks and threatens to undermine the very structure on which the industry
is based.

The likelihood that one or more such challengers will
appear is a strong one. In fact, it appears that such would-be
contenders for control of the real estate transaction may
already be on the horizon.

These potential combatants realize that whoever estab-
lishes and maintains initial contact with the home-buying

and/or home-selling consumer is in a position to control a vast array of activities connected with the purchase or sale of a parcel of real estate. Inspections, warranties, furnishings and fixtures, landscaping, mortgage financing, escrow activities, title search, title insurance, attorney services, moving and storage, temporary housing and insurance are some of the areas where business can be directed, if not controlled, by the initiator of the property-buying and property-selling process.

And then, of course, there are the two truly big ones—the sale itself and the mortgage financing attached thereto.

Historically, a progressive real estate brokerage firm has been at the controls for much, if not all, of this activity. It is the manifestation of the one-stop shopping concept.

Yet it need not continue to be so!

Nothing in the process of buying and selling property dictates that a real estate practitioner must be at the vortex of the vast aforementioned array of activity.

Perhaps the first to see the possibility of replacing the real estate brokerage at the center of activity is the mortgage banking industry.

Advertising campaigns undertaken by members of the Mortgage Banking Association (MBA) that advise "Get your loan first" are somewhat more than a consumer service suggestion. They are an attempt to establish initial contact with purchasers and, having done so, refer them to vendors and suppliers of the various other goods and services connected with the transaction—including real estate brokerage.

Increasingly, mortgage bankers see themselves reversing the traditional process. No longer, they think, must a buyer flow from a real estate agent to a financier. It can go in the other direction.

No wonder banners are seen at MBA meetings proclaiming, "Soon, the REALTORS® will be sponsoring our golf tournaments."

The real estate community will not yield quietly and serenely to such threats. It will look for ways both in the marketplace and in the legislative and judicial arenas to prevent intrusion into what has traditionally been regarded as the REALTOR®s' private domain. Moreover, the opposition of the real estate industry to competitive intrusions by mortgage bankers will not be limited to defensive maneuvers. As the financiers attempt to move into real estate, so will the real estate brokers be attempting to expand into mortgage banking, either through a route of direct ownership or through alliances with established mortgage lenders.

The confrontation is likely to be lengthy, costly and, oftentimes, ugly.

And mortgage banking may not be the only battleground. Any number of other commercial enterprises could, at the drop of a hat, decide to marshal resources for an intrusion into real estate brokerage.

Those who think otherwise point to the fruitless attempts of major retailers (such as Sears) or insurance enterprises (such as Metropolitan) or securities dealers (e.g., Thompson McKinnon and Merrill Lynch) to expand into real estate brokerage. But their historic argument is largely shattered by the agility and forcefulness demonstrated by the actions of HFS (a company that prior to its 1995 purchase of the Century 21 franchise, was never heard of in real estate circles) in establishing not only a competitive, but, some say, a dominant position in the industry with suddenness and briskness. HFS now controls somewhere between 23 percent and 27 percent of all residential resale transactions through one or another of its franchised brands. (For a detailed explanation of HFS and its affect on the real estate industry, see Chapter 3.)

It could easily happen again. And this time it could be an entrant that, unlike HFS, would not operate within the realm of traditional real estate brokerage, but rather with a totally different approach—one designed to replace the brokerage industry rather than operate within it. All that is needed is determination, direction and abundant resources, especially of a financial nature.

Likely suspects as potential "invaders" of the real estate industry's "turf" are corporate technological entities (such as Microsoft), information enterprises (especially publishers and telecommunications) and even retailers (yes, again!).

If and when they all appear on the scene, singly or as multiple intruders, the real estate community will look for a means of banding together to ward them off. Under such circumstances, the National Association of REALTORS® is the natural rallying point.

So, it may well be that wars with external forces will be the unifying force that brings peace (or at least détente) to the internal factionalism that might otherwise cause considerable damage to the NAR.

Even so, just as historical major armed confrontations have produced lasting changes to victor and vanquished alike, so too will the competitive battles of the future (be they external or internal) severely alter the form and structure of "organized real estate."

The NAR of the future will not be the same as it is now, but it will be!

CHAPTER 3

HFS: Cash! Catalyst!? Committed!?

"We were never in the lodging business just as we never intend to be in the real estate business. What we are in is the franchise business—a business that we think we know pretty well."

Henry Silverman, Chairman and CEO, HFS

It could stand for "Homes For Sale." In fact, when it first made its appearance on the real estate scene in 1995, many otherwise knowledgeable real estate agents probably thought that was as good a guess as any for what was behind the letters *HFS.*

They now know better.

HFS (originally known as Hospitality Franchise Systems) is involved in selling homes all right, but en route to that end goal it is dramatically changing the real estate industry. And soon it will be changing its name—again!

In less than two years (beginning with its purchase of Century 21 in August 1995), this actively traded New York Stock Exchange Company with soaring price levels gained control of residential real estate companies, commanding between 23 percent and 27 percent of the total housing resale market.

It did so in a series of industry-shaking acquisition moves by acquiring, in rapid succession, three major franchise organizations—Century 21 and ERA in February 1996 and Coldwell Banker in May 1996. In all, the trio brought to HFS more than 11,000 office locations, 210,000 agents and about one million unit transactions per year with a total sales volume in the range of $150 trillion.

Even then, HFS had not concluded its foray into the real estate industry. In what most observers consider its most significant transaction to date, in April 1997 it acquired PHH Inc., itself a tripart corporate giant with commanding positions in corporate relocation management, home mortgage financing and automobile and related leasing operations.

Then they went and did it again it again! Just when it looked as though the company was going to give itself some breathing room to absorb the recent $1.7 billion acquisition of PHH, it startled the experts by coming forth with a true merger arrangement that is likely to dramatically restructure the company, if not the real estate industry as well.

HFS has joined forces with CUC International, Inc., a company best known for its coupon books and traveler and shopper-membership clubs (typically charging members an annual fee for the right to purchase goods and services at discount rates) in what officials of both firms are calling a "genuine merger with a tax-free exchange of shares." The combined company, to be named Cendant, Inc. at the closing of the transaction, expected in the last quarter of 1997, will be a leading provider of consumer and business services worldwide. It would have had combined revenues of approximately $4.3 billion, net income of nearly $600 million and free cash flow of approximately $700 million based on pro forma performance in calendar 1996, and a market capitalization of approximately $22 billion. CUC began as CompU-Card of America in 1973 and has grown into a leading member services and direct marketing organization offering value and convenience to consumers in shopping, travel, dining, local merchant discounts, auto and home buying and many other services, with over 68 million memberships worldwide. Cross-marketing opportunities between the two companies are expected to increase further revenue and profit growth for the merged enterprise.

Like its soon-to-be partner, CUC Inc. has also remained active following the HFS merger announcement. In early August, 1997, it signed a definitive share purchase agreement to acquire the privately held Hebdo Mag. The new acquisition, formerly privately held, is a major publisher of periodicals specializing in classified advertising, with more than 150 publications and 200 million readers in 12 countries throughout the globe. The firm is headquartered in Paris.

In announcing the acquisition, Walter A. Forbes, chairman and chief executive officer of CUC Inc. stated, "This is a good strategic fit as classified advertisements are integral to our goal of reaching consumers just before every significant purchasing decision they make.

"We will be able to expand our current classified offerings to include used cars, boats, *real estate,* computers and employment. With CUC's existing consumer services and HFS's preferred alliances, we will now be able to leverage our direct-marketing expertise to cross-sell complementary services, such as AutoVantage, to someone buying a car."

Following the merger with CUC, HFS chairman and CEO Henry Silverman will serve as president and CEO of the combined company. Forbes will be chairman of the board of directors. On January 1, 2000, Forbes will become president and CEO and Silverman will become chairman. John D. Snodgrass, vice chairman, president and COO of HFS, and Stephen P. Holmes, Robert D. Kunisch and Michael P. Monaco, each vice chairmen of HFS, will also serve as vice chairmen of the combined company. The two companies will maintain their operations in Parsippany, New Jersey, home of HFS, and Stamford, Connecticut, where CUC is headquartered, as well as New York and other locations. It

is not expected that there will be any reductions in employment at either company as a result of this transaction.

For the year ended January 31, 1997, CUC reported revenues of $2.3 billion. HFS reported net income of $283 million and earnings per share of $0.70. Including PHH, which
was acquired in 1997 as a pooling of interests, HFS had pro
forma revenues of approximately $2 billion and pro forma
net income of $309 million, or $1.75 per share.

Moreover, according to such HFS leaders as Silverman,
the massive conglomerate is not yet calling a halt to its
"growth through acquisition" spree. "We are a company
that is always in an acquisitive mode," Silverman notes.
"This merger just gives us twice as many resources to use in
expanding." Snodgrass is a bit more specific with respect to
the real estate industry. "Most of our activity is likely to be
in pursuing additional acquisitions in fields ancillary to real
estate, such as mortgage banking and corporate relocation,"
he explains, "but we could explore the notion of a fourth
real estate brand."

Such statements confirm the opinion of veteran real
estate observers that the industry has seen nothing resembling this type of whirlwind activity in its recorded history.
Previous attempts of major business enterprises such as
Sears, Merrill Lynch, TWA, Control Data and Metropolitan
Insurance to penetrate the real estate brokerage industry
pale in comparison with HFS's thrust onto the scene.

What has made the company's undertakings all the more
spectacular is the speed with which they have been
achieved—that, and the resources that HFS has deployed in
reaching those achievements. In all, prior to the CUC
announcement, the aggregate purchase prices of the three
franchise groups plus PHH is in the general vicinity of $3.4
billion. And that's not all! To expand the number of brokerage offices affiliated with one or another of its franchise
brands, HFS (through an independent vehicle called the
National Realty Trust) has spent another sizable sum to
acquire such previously independent firms as the 33-office

Burgdorff REALTORS®, in New Jersey; the 18-office Contempo Realty, in northern California; the 5-facility Kahn Realty, in suburban Chicago; and several other well-positioned brokerages.

Some of the purchases (such as PHH) have been financed through HFS stock, but regardless of the method of exchange used, they represent a massive commitment of financial resources.

WHIRLWIND OF ACTIVITY IS NOTHING NEW TO HFS

While this type of whirlwind activity is startling to the real estate industry, it is nothing new to HFS. Incorporated in May 1990, HFS had its first public offering of common stock in December 1992. Its initial price was $4 per share. The company was originally known as Hospitality Franchise Systems.

Almost anyone watching at the time would have identified the company as a new entrant in the lodging field. Indeed, Hospitality Franchise Systems' expressed interest certainly seemed to be in the motel field, because it was the franchisor of record for eight well-recognized lodging brands with an aggregate of 500,000 rooms. All such observers would not have been precisely on target, however. As Silverman is quick to note, "We were never in the lodging business just as we never intend to be in the real estate business. What we are in is the franchise business—a business that we think we know pretty well."

It was, therefore, as a franchisor, not as an owner/operator, that Hospitality Franchise Systems came to have under its wing the franchise rights to such national motel brands as Days Inn, Ramada, Howard Johnson, Super 8, Travelodge, Villager Lodge, Knights Inn and Wingate Inn by 1995 when it first became involved with real estate brokerage. But, when his company undertook its initial acquisition in that arena (Century 21), Silverman looked upon that move not as entering a new field of endeavor, but rather as an expansion of the company's basic business of franchising.

Even after its presence in the real estate field was well established, HFS continued its expansion into other franchise areas, acquiring Avis Rent-A-Car in late 1996. It entered into an agreement to acquire Value Car Rental but withdrew during due diligence studies.

Two other recent purchases—Resorts Condominiums International and PHH—will test the HFS philosophy of being a franchisor first, last and always because each has been strictly a corporately owned and operated enterprise. Even if they remain so, it can be said that one of the principal justifications for their acquisitions is their ability to blend their services synergistically with and through the HFS franchise organizations.

Blending together company operations with CUC will also present new challenges, because CUC operations are outside the realm of franchising. Yet they are not too far distant, inasmuch as CUC has a revenue base of membership dues (not unlike franchise fees, except in amounts) and a cadre of vendors rendering fees for the opportunity to serve that membership base (not unlike HFS's preferred vendor alliances). Moreover, it is likely that CUC will have and receive distinct contributions from cross-selling opportunities with the franchised units.

The following are among the criss-cross opportunities the new company is excepted to provide in the real estate field:

- Linking HFS's one million annual home buyers and sellers, served by Coldwell Banker, Century 21 and ERA, with CUC's Complete Home Service, which provides home improvement, repair and upkeep information, a referral database of more than 8,000 contractors and tradespeople; and other services for homeowners. CUC's direct marketing capability will dramatically increase the combined company's ability to assist these consumers in the numerous purchasing decisions typically made by new home buyers or such topics as health care providers, dry cleaners, house painting, hardware, repair services and more.

- Combining HFS's industry-leading corporate relocation service, which assists 100,000 employees and their families per year, with CUC's New Mover services, such as Welcome Wagon, Getting to Know You and Entertainment, which provide coupons and offers from local merchants to new residents.
- Combining CUC's industry-leading capability for online transactions with HFS's leading brands. For example, CUC's successful electronic real estate classified service, RentNet, could serve as a model for application to HFS-brand web sites, such as Coldwell Banker's and Century 21's.
- The aforementioned use of Hebdo Mag publications to extend the reach of real estate classified advertising nationally.

Staying within the confines of franchising was no problem for HFS in its acquisitions of Century 21 and ERA. In each case, every office within the network was licensed under a franchise agreement. Coldwell Banker presented a different case. The 90-year-old West Coast company brought to the merger table not only 2,200 franchised offices, but also 325 company-owned facilities, most of which were flying under the Coldwell Banker banner as a result of independent regional megabrokers having sold to Coldwell Banker in the decade or so preceding HFS's entry into the real estate arena.

Using the creativity that had enabled it to grow from a thinly capitalized start-up company in the mid 1980s to a marvel of Wall Street in the mid 1990s, HFS solved the non-ownership dilemma by establishing an entity called the National Realty Trust for the purpose of buying, owning and operating the company-owned offices, endowing it with sufficient capital to consummate the purchase and establishing it as a wholly independent entity with its own board of directors with Chandler Barton as its chairman. Barton had been chairman and CEO of Coldwell Banker. The trust was vested with the responsibility to continue acquiring independent companies that could then enter into a franchised relationship with one of the three HFS brands while at the same time staying abreast of the opportunity to divest itself of holdings if such a maneuver would ameliorate another HFS purchase or franchise addition.

But HFS is not a company committed to "status quoism." It had no intention for the National Realty Trust to be simply a reservoir of independent companies that elected to sell to the giant conglomerate rather than franchise. Instead it saw the trust as a catalyst for continuing growth by being actively engaged in the acquisition of numerous companies that, together with vibrant franchising activity, would establish a massive market share in record-shattering time.

The efforts have been far more than moderately successful. In not quite one year of operation, the number of companies owned by the National Realty Trust expanded to 380. Of that number, 30 are ERA franchisees, 18 belong to Century 21, and the remainder are members of Coldwell Banker.

In addition to Coldwell Banker, the most well-known acquisitions are those of the New Jersey–based 33-office Burgdorff REALTORS®, for the ERA network, and northern California's 18-office Contempo Realty, entering the Century 21 franchise. Each of these acquisitions received widespread industry attention because they were connected with arrangements that brought new presidents to ERA and Century 21. Peter Burgdorff, former owner and CEO of the realty firm bearing his name, became president of ERA in mid-1996, filling the office vacated since the departure of very-short-term president Fred Beilstein earlier that year. Contempo's president and founder, Robert T. "Bob" Moles, came with the sale of his company in March 1997 to assume the presidency of Century 21, which had been vacant since the sudden departure of effervescent former CEO Robert "Bob" Pittman for a top executive post at America Online in late 1996.

In consummating both of these transactions, HFS appeared to be accomplishing two highly desirable goals at the same time: adding a much-needed presence of a well-respected national megabrokerage to the ranks of franchises otherwise mostly characterized by smaller firms and filling the franchise presidencies with men who command respect as experienced real estate practitioners and can "talk the language" of the real estate community.

Although industry attention has been focused on the three major acquisitions of the trust, by no means does the trio constitute the totality of acquisition activity. Since its inception with the Coldwell Banker transaction, the trust has purchased a number of interesting companies, including Kahn Realty, with 5 offices and 325 sales associates, in the North Shore area of Chicagoland; Del Monte Realty, a 5-office, 65-agent firm on the Monterey Peninsula in northern California; Neal and Neal REALTORS®, in the Bradenton, Florida, area, a firm with 5 offices and 90 associates; and Marie Powell Realty, a multiple-office firm in the St. Petersburg, Florida, area, headed by a former president of the Florida Association of REALTORS®. All affiliated with Coldwell Banker. At any given time, the trust also seems to be working on numerous additional acquisitions, many of them appearing to be nearing consummation, along with a number of smaller transactions also on the docket.

Thus far, when a multioffice firm has been acquired by the National Realty Trust, all of its offices have joined the same franchise, each signing an independent franchise agreement, with the length of the agreement in synch with all the other offices of the same firm. Such a procedure need not be the case in the future.

Actually, when the trust acquires a real estate organization, it has all the normal rights of ownership. Thus, it could split up the offices among the three HFS brands, consolidate the offices, or even sell some or all of them if conditions warranted. In some situations, however, terms of the acquisition might commit the trust to follow a stable and defined pattern of operation for a period of time.

"What must be understood," according to Robert Arrigoni, president of the trust from its inception until mid-1997, "is the fact that the National Realty Trust needs to be financially sound in its own right. So, it must look for acquisitions that will contribute to that soundness as they blend into the culture of both the trust and the particular franchise with which they will be associated."

"By the same token," he continued, "HFS is committed to the fiscal growth and prosperity of its shareholders, so it too is very concerned about the quality of firms being acquired by the trust and by the proper alignment of the firm within the franchise groups after it is acquired."

Thus, he conjectured, the National Realty Trust could acquire a 15-office company, and align 5 of the locations with Coldwell Banker, another 5 with Century 21 and a final 5 with ERA.

Established as a "totally independent" business entity, in its original concept, The National Realty Trust was funded by HFS to an extent required to conclude desired acquisitions. Once up and running, however, through the successful operation of its ownership holdings, the enterprise itself was expected to render a profit. HFS's immediate "take" from the trust was in the form of normal franchise fees paid by each entity within the trust, with one exception. Whereas large franchisees within the Coldwell Banker and Century 21 franchises may receive a financial rebate, often of some substantial amount once they reach various levels of royalty fee payments, all of the National Realty Trust holdings are expected to pay the full franchise fee, regardless of their production volume.

In summer 1997, the National Realty Trust underwent substantive changes in top executive personnel. Robert M. "Bob" Becker moved over from the presidency of the Coldwell Banker franchise brand to assume a similar post as CEO of The Trust (He was succeeded at Coldwell Banker by veteran corporate executive Alex Perriello). The adjustment in personnel was the forerunner of a total restructuring of HFS's approach to indirectly "acquiring" companies. In mid-August, 1997, the company, in effect, finalized plans to terminate the National Realty Trust, and transpose its functions to a new independent entity—NRT Inc., which it identified as "a venture created to acquire residential real estate brokerage firms."

NRT Inc.'s first acquisition was the assets of the National Realty Trust, viz., the nearly 400 residential real estate firms franchised under either the Century 21, Coldwell Banker or ERA banner. Joining with HFS in the information—and ownership—of NRT Inc. is Apollo Management L.P., a private investment partnership which has invested $7 billion in a variety of real estate and corporate transactions since its founding by Leon D. Black in 1990.

To launch the new enterprise HFS invested $157 million in senior and convertible preferred stock of NRT Inc. with Apollo and other institutions contributing $75 million for 100% of the common and junior preferred stock. Initially, NRT Inc. will have approximately $575 million in cash and committed funds with which to pursue acquisitions. It is reported that NRT Inc. will bring to conclusion a number of preliminary agreements originated by National Realty Trust that had been awaiting definitive documentaion and other "due diligence" procedures. All NRT Inc. acquisitions will be franchised within the HFS portfolio of holdings. In addition, NRT Inc. will contract with PHH Mortgage Services (another HFS Division) to be the sole mortgage originator within all its offices. Becker moves from the post of president and chief executive officer of National Realty Trust to the same posts in NRT Inc. Barton shifts from the chairmanship of the Trust to chairmanship of NRT Inc. Other senior executives of National Realty Trust assume parallel positions with the new company.

As one key executive describes the shift from the National Realty Trust to NRT Inc., "The arm's length relationship between HFS and its 'acquisition arm' just grew several yards longer."

Though perhaps more distant, HFS will continue to have an intense interest in NRT Inc. activities. In a pure physical sense, it will be able to do so easily because NRT Inc. will be headquartered in Parsippany, New Jersey, the home of HFS rather than the Mission Viejo, California site of the National Realty Trust.

Becker, a native New Jersian, has promoted a host of individuals to vice presidencies and regional directorships previously held by personnel based in the former California headquarters who declined to relocate. Even more important than these personnel moves, however, was the fact that when the company moved, neither Arrigoni nor Barton moved with it.

Barton's position as chairman of the board does not require him to be involved in daily operational details of NRT. Thus, he can function efficiently from virtually any location. He is choosing to do so from two—southern California, where he maintains his office in the former Coldwell Banker headquarters building; and Atlanta, the city where Barton established an erstwhile reputation as CEO of Barton and Ludwig REALTORS®, an early acquisition by Coldwell Banker, and a place that he still considers home. Other than not being in a location proximate to the operational staff, Barton's position and role in the National Realty Trust remains virtually unchanged by the move. He continues to preside at board meetings, is available for sage consultation and direction whenever needed and on call for assists in bringing to closure especially challenging acquisition transactions.

Arrigoni's was a much different situation.

Enamored with the climate and culture of his native state, he rejected the opportunity to go to New Jersey with NRT Inc. and instead resigned from the presidency.

After an intensive interview and evaluation process, in June 1997, HFS replaced Arrigoni with Becker, who, prior to his service as president and CEO of the Coldwell Banker franchise, was president and COO for Coldwell Banker Schlott REALTORS®, a company he joined in 1980 (when it was know as Schlott REALTORS®) after it purchased the Mountain Lakes, New Jersey, company his mother had started in the early 1960s.

His successor, Perriello, in addition to a long term of service with Coldwell Banker, starting as a sales agent 14 years ago, was one of the few top personnel to transfer from that company's former California headquarters to HFS's Parsippany site.

Despite his unwillingness to transfer, Arrigoni sees the restructuring and relocation of the acquisition company as a prudent business decision. "Needless to say, from my personal perspective I would like to have seen things stay put in California," he admits. "But when HFS, the principal financier and business collaborator of NRT Inc., is in New Jersey, it doesn't make much sense for us to be nearly 3,000 miles away."

"Frankly," he adds, "were I in another, earlier segment of my career, I would have made the move, but I have deep family and personal roots where I am and, fortunately for me, the financial aspect of the Coldwell Banker sale to HFS was highly beneficial."

"Everything in NRT Inc. will not stay exactly the same as it was in the National Realty Trust," Arrigoni predicts. "For one thing," he adds, "since virtually everybody working for the trust in California was a former Coldwell Banker employee, Coldwell Banker culture was sort of ingrained into the trust. Now, it's a fine culture, but HFS transcends a whole host of enterprises, including three real estate brands and now, in PHH, a major company aligned to the real estate profession. I suspect with new personnel on hand, there may well be a wider scope of organizational culture and background in NRT Inc. and this will be good for all concerned."

The fulfillment of Arrigoni's predictions may be vital to the success of NRT Inc. Now that both ERA and Century 21 have well respected men with solid real estate backgrounds at their helm in the persons of Burgdorff at ERA and Moles at Century 21, it seems likely that these two leaders will want to see vibrant activity on the part of NRT Inc., leading to the expansion of their franchises as well as that of Coldwell Banker.

THE BROKERAGE INDUSTRY RESPONDS TO HFS

The aggressiveness of HFS's expansion moves, both through NRT Inc. and in directly acquiring additional representatives for its brands through franchise sales, has taken the real estate industry by storm.

Some independent brokerage firms have responded by offering themselves as candidates for further HFS acquisition. Others have explored the mechanics and the finances of franchise affiliation either with an HFS brand or a competitor.

Then there are those who consider HFS as a worthy but dauntless challenger and who are restructuring their own strategies and tactics to offset the presence of this new participant in competitive combat.

Overall, whether they are calculating "how we can fight 'em" or "how we can join 'em," thousands of real estate brokers/owners are conjecturing their futures with HFS very much on their minds.

Joining the HFS family of companies is especially attractive to some brokers/owners because of the financial aspects they perceive to be attached to such a move. The reality of industry conditions in the late 1990s are such that there is good reason to believe that even amid strong market conditions, many brokerage firms, large and small, find it difficult to realize a profit. Some analysts are convinced that fully 30 to 50 percent of real estate firms do not make money on their brokerage. If they survive and prosper, it is a result of activities ancillary to brokerage, such as property management, insurance, mortgage origination, warranties, title and escrow companies and the like.

Because of such conditions, some independent broker firms have been reveling in the notion that HFS pays top dollar (and perhaps then some) for its acquisitions. Possibly so, but close examination suggests that even though the sums of money involved in some acquisitions are sizable, HFS has been quite shrewd in such financial matters. For one thing, many HFS purchases have been, in whole or in part, paid for with company stock. Merger of the new enterprise into the HFS entity has almost always been followed immediately by an increase in market value of HFS stock, significantly increasing the company's market capitalization. Thus, in effect, HFS has been paying for these types of acquisitions with the added value brought to it by the acquisition.

Additionally, in the specific cases of the three real estate franchises, HFS saw itself as being able to increase operational efficiencies by spreading similar "back office" operations and the cost connected therewith across a broader unit base. Moreover, by increasing its overall office and agent population and by dramatically expanding its consumer contact, HFS was establishing a structure for a major expansion of "affiliate" and "affinity" relationships with a wide variety of vendors who render considerable license fees (nearly $70 million in the aggregate in 1997) to HFS for the right to sell to or through its franchised outlets.

Whatever the rationale, early sellers to the National Realty Trust and to HFS received payments considerably in excess of what had until then been prevailing standards in the real estate industry. Leading evaluators of the market value of real estate firms contend that they increased 50 to

60 percent because of HFS's activities. Subsequently, of course, other sellers expect the same kind of financial consideration. As Richard Smith, president of HFS's Real Estate Division, puts it, "The industry is inundated with independent firms that either want to exit the business or grow their firm with someone else's capital."

Those who contemplate a franchise affiliation have similar notions. Increasingly, they see the franchisor (i.e., ultimately, HFS) providing extensive financial assistance to the "conversion process" from independent to franchisee. Whether such resources are extended in the form of a grant, a loan or some combination thereof, independent firms coming aboard one of HFS's enterprises expect the immediate cost thereof to be extensive, and they expect to pay little or none of it.

If they are successful in receiving such start-up largesse, it will be because HFS sees long-term benefits in the relationship that more than justify their initial investment.

PHH SEEN AS A "GREAT BUY," EVEN AT $1.8 BILLION

In like manner, HFS obviously saw sufficient merit in the acquisition of PHH to account for the approximately $1.8 billion (in HFS stock) that it paid for the company. In short, that merit might be labeled "optimal synergy."

Each of PHH's three business divisions—corporate relocation management, mortgage financing and leasing (especially auto leasing)—has a natural interplay with one or more HFS divisions. In addition, there is a significant challenge and, potentially, a major opportunity for the National Realty Trust evolving from consummation of HFS' purchase of PHH. One of the three major divisions of PHH's business endeavors was Relocation Management Services. In connection therewith, the company was responsible for annually assisting thousands of corporate transferees in disposing of one home and acquiring another, usually in another part of the country. In doing so, PHH acted on behalf of its corporate clients—the companies that are transferring the employees.

To assist in these activities, PHH had enlisted a cadre of top-flight brokerage firms across the nation, the vast majority of which are independent megabrokers. The disposition of this PHH network of brokers following the closing of the sale to HFS is cause for much conjecture within the real estate industry and considerable concern among the members of the network, HFS executives and franchisees in the three HFS networks.

PHH network members have been nervous lest HFS redirect its PHH-client-based business exclusively—or mostly—to members of the three franchises.

The franchisees are troubled lest HFS continue to award former PHH client business to the nonfranchised megabrokers.

HFS executives anxiously examined how they might retain the goodwill and ongoing business of the PHH corporate clients without unduly upsetting either the franchisees or the megabrokers.

Actually, the executives have a model for the ideal situation and would be delighted if they achieved it, viz., convince all of the megabrokerage members of the PHH network that they should combine forces with HFS by joining one or another of the HFS franchise brands or, as a second option, sell to the National Realty Trust so that it could then reposition the megabrokerage offices into one of the franchises.

Because the odds against realization of this optimal fantasy are rather astronomical, HFS and the National Realty Trust appear to be opting for the next best thing—to convince the independent PHH megabrokers (and others) that they are not adversarial to real estate enterprises outside their spheres of ownership and, at all costs, to avoid an appearance of arrogance or haughtiness.

Good evidence of this approach was Snodgrass's comment immediately preceding the 1997 PHH annual convention in Hawaii that he was going to the conference "to listen and to learn" and to convince other attendees of HFS's commitment to continue to use the "best of the best" in the real estate brokerage community to service PHH corporate clients and their transferees.

From all reports he succeeded admirably.

Without doubt, a goodly number of attendees were on hand for one or more of the following reasons:

- To object to certain PHH policies
- To learn of precise plans that HFS has for PHH following completion of the acquisition
- To argue with HFS personnel over the direction it might be charting for PHH
- To chart a corporate strategy for their firms that would convert them from collaborators with PHH to competitors with PHH/HFS

They were disappointed on all scores. What ensued in Hawaii was more like "business as usual" with Snodgrass and Smith carefully and diplomatically attempting to convince broker delegates of HFS's desire and need to work with them for everyone's welfare and advancement. Reportedly, any anticipated arguments and competitive strategies were supplanted by friendliness and understanding as everyone got to know one another.

Obviously, HFS would like to chart a course through the horns of a dilemma currently on the horizon—whether to direct PHH client business to franchisees, thereby running the risk of forever losing any goodwill (and possible merger notions) on the part of the independent megabrokers and possibly alienating the corporate client base; or continue to convey PHH business to current members of the PHH network and encounter the hostility of franchisees who would feel "sold out" by their own franchisor.

HFS appears to be pursuing a solution that, though not optimal, may be the most realistically realizeable—bring enough megabrokers into the HFS family that the company can justifiably claim that it (1) respects the rights of franchisees and (2) plans to continue the client-megabroker relationship that has long existed in PHH. But, at the same time, through a qualitative upgrading of personnel and skills within its franchised brands, it will try to convince corporate clients that enough of "the best of the best" operate under one or another HFS banner to justify the placing of meaningful relocation business with them. In addition, one characteristic that HFS may evaluate in determining "the best of the best" may be whether they direct their mortgage loan activity to PHH.

The company began this delicate process shortly after the April 30, 1997 closing of the PHH transaction by combining PHH, Coldwell Banker Relocation Services (acquired by HFS at the time of the Coldwell Banker takeover) and Worldwide Relocation (which came to HFS via the Century 21 purchase, where it was once known as Western Relocation) into one entity, calling it HFS Mobility Services. Named to president and CEO offices in the new organization was Kevin Kelleher, veteran executive with PHH who most recently was senior vice president for PHH Relocation. He will report to Richard Smith, president of the HFS real estate division, and thus be a direct part of the brokerage operations. Although in his acceptance remarks Kelleher said, "In launching HFS Mobility Services, we will capitalize on the best practices developed by each of the three companies over the past four decades," most observers expected the PHH modus operandi to prevail in most areas.

While HFS seeks a route through the horns of the PHH dilemma, its competitors and adversaries are doing their best to strew that path with what they hope will be insurmountable roadblocks. Most noticeable activity has been undertaken by Genesis Relocation Services, a top-ranked relocation network of leading independent brokers.

In a direct countermeasure to HFS's acquisition of PHH and formation of HFS Mobility Services, Genesis has joined forces with The Realty Alliance (a newly formed consortium of major independent firms—covered in detail in Chapter 4) to form an international referral network and relocation services company that they are calling "Reliance Relocation Services." In explaining the move to members, Genesis President John M. Moore writes, "Consolidation within both the real estate and relocation industries, continued downsizing among the ranks of middle management in American corporations, and, *most important, the opportunities which are likely to be created by the HFS/PHH* merger were among the trends which prompted us to consider alternatives to or current structure, ownership and capitalization. Coincidentally, members of The Realty Alliance were simultaneously considering similar options. We are trying to ensure that the members of our new organization will have the ability to remain in control of their relocation business as well as help them increase their relocation business over time." There is no assurance that all of the 50-odd megabrokers in the ranks of the Realty Alliance will support the new company (and thus place their PHH relationship in a precarious position). Moore believes that between 30 and 35 of the group will join the Reliance Relocation Service early on, and, quite possibly, more later.

HFS continues to stress that it will service the needs of its corporate mobility clients with "the best of the best" broker representatives, be they franchisees or independents.

HFS'S INTERESTS GO FAR BEYOND REAL ESTATE

Whenever one considers the impact of HFS on the real estate brokerage industry, it is easy to lose sight of the fact that the company controlled by Henry Silverman has other interests beyond real estate. It is a serious mistake to do so. Silverman's expansions from the base of lodging franchises that launched HFS (nee Hospitality Franchise Systems) have consistently been to establish synergy, cross-selling and mutual profit enhancement among all of the facets of the HFS empire.

And so it well might continue to be, enlarging the overall corporate coffers of HFS beyond anyone's vivid imagination, if the company is able to bring all the somewhat disparate parts together while at the same time sustaining a desirable high rate of return on each. After all, as Silverman has said many times, "We are not in the lodging business. We are not in the real estate business. And we are not in the auto rental business. We are in the franchise business." And, as he has thoughtfully added, "We are in any business at all to maximize value for our shareholders." (It might well be noted that Silverman himself is one of those shareholders—a substantial one.) Now, with the CUC transaction, that goal—and challenge—is all the more intense, especially since some Wall Street analysts are contending that the merged enterprise will be too big and highly capitalized to increase earnings growth at a commendable rate.

To generate hundreds of millions of dollars by cross-selling motel rooms, houses, condominium time shares, auto rentals, real estate mortgages and, now, buyer club memberships requires two things—a large prospective customer base and substantial control of that customer base by making sure it is amenable to the idea of a single source contact for all of the above, or at least a single point of reference.

The prospect numbers are there—and then some! Add together the number of persons who sleep in one of the 500,000 hotel and motel beds operating under an HFS brand; the company's 25 percent or so market share of the nearly eight million individuals involved annually in a home purchase sale or purchase; the several hundred thousand who rent, lease or swap an RCI time-sharing unit; the multitude who rent cars from Avis; the army of transferees relocating with assistance from top relocation management companies; the vast array of mortgagors who have financed their homes through PHH; the untold throngs of consumers attracted to an HFS entity because of the company's affiliation with nearly 80 alliance vendors; and now, the 68 million members of CUC buying clubs spread around the world; and you have a figure capable of testing the capacity of highly sophisticated calculators.

Such a superfluity of potential customers accentuates the enormity of directing that horde of individuals to HFS products. It is no wonder that Snodgrass has stated that "Finding a way to mine our database of prospects is one of the greatest challenges we face." Or that Silverman has frequently observed that among HFS potential future acquisitions targets are "established direct marketing companies."

Both statements were uttered prior to the CUC merger. Obviously, HFS found what it was looking for!

Yet, it continues to search for more. From all accounts, HFS was close to acquiring The Signature Group, a direct marketing subsidiary of the Montgomery Ward Group, but altered its bid after Montgomery Ward filed for bankruptcy protection for all of its operations except The Signature Group. Montgomery Ward rejected the revised offer as being inadequate.

Not every participant in the real estate brokerage community responds to the HFS onslaught by trying to climb aboard the juggernaut. Many consider the presence of this new challenger to be a stimulant to more innovative and progressive activity on their own part.

But whatever strategy they ultimately follow, the challenges and opportunities presented by HFS are so vast and all-encompassing that they are impacting on the motives and motivations of virtually every major independent brokerage firm and national realty organization, including the following areas of dominant HFS influence:

- Growth through acquisition. As it set the pace with its absorptions of Century 21, ERA, Coldwell Banker, PHH, RCI and the like, HFS has alerted numerous independents to the notion that a "buy" strategy for expansion may be much preferred to a "make" approach and that, in any event, market share and economies of scale are directly connected with size of operation.
- With more than 100 affinity and preferred vendor alliances now in place throughout its total organization, HFS has established a system of additional income streams and expanded distribution now being emulated in every segment of the real estate community as firms large and small grapple to establish meaningful relationships leading to additional business opportunities.
- Through its union with CUC, HFS will set the pace for industrywide realization of the effectiveness of proper "database mining." Few, if any, competitors have access to the nearly 100 million consumer records available to HFS. Yet all have some potentially meaningful lists. HFS is alerting them to the idea that "what's in a name" is in direct relationship to what you do with that name in add-on marketing, cross-selling and repetitive business opportunities.
- With its acquisition of PHH, HFS has so reshuffled the relocation facet of the real estate business that full ramification will be not be properly evaluated for quite some time. Already, however, other brokerage groups, referral networks, relocation management companies and client corporations are all reevaluating their options in lieu of the HFS/PHH merger and subsequent consolidation of all HFS relocation into a single entity. The new entity started by Genesis and the Realty Alliance may not be the last of the "Counter-HFS" moves.
- The sheer magnitude and swiftness of HFS's actions have caused many firms to realize that "in unity there is strength" and to seek alliances or working partner-

ships with other brokerage firms of similar size and operation. The Realty Alliance itself is one such notable union combining two long-standing informal idea-sharing groups—the Masterminds and the Dozen—into one expanded network now consisting of 51 megabrokerage firms regularly sharing ideas and resources and planning to undertake a number of coventured activities. (Chapter 4 examines the Realty Alliance in greater detail.)

The remainder of the real estate world would be making a mistake if it went to either extreme regarding HFS—either conjecturing that it is a meteoric entity that will ultimately crash with the same swiftness that it has soared or that it is destined to be of such gargantuan size and strength as to rapidly establish an oligopoly that, in effect, will virtually control the destiny of the real estate industry and all its practitioners.

A much more realistic appraisal is to evaluate what HFS is doing and will do in the future, viz., hone the overall competitiveness of the industry and force all participants to refashion their operations to win public acceptance by rendering what consumers perceive to be greater value and service.

Without doubt, when new concepts and approaches are introduced in the real estate business, there is a ripple effect throughout much of the industry. But the ripple can—and should—activate others in the profession to recalculate their own strategies and refashion their own sense of direction.

Not all will be successful.

But enough will to ensure a real estate industry of the future that is more professional, more efficient and, definitely, more attuned to the peculiarities of a new century and a new millennium.

That such conditions will exist is evident from perusing a number of other leading entities in the real estate industry. The next chapter will do so in detail.

CHAPTER 4

Chasing Number 1

"All the fun and pleasure has been taken out of real estate."

anonymous independent broker

Most examinations of what is happening or about to happen in the residential real estate brokerage industry draw an immediate distinction between the independents and the franchised firms. There is validity in such categorization because, to a certain extent, companies do attune themselves to different drummers depending upon whether their march through the business is in unison with others or undertaken as a solo performance. While real estate franchised firms do not clone themselves after a master model in the same manner as a McDonald's outlet or a Holiday Inn, there is nonetheless an attempt to effect some similarity of operation among the members of the franchise. This tendency toward sameness is perhaps most apparent in advertising and promotion where, for the most part, franchised firms tend to present the same messages in the same manner, hoping to capitalize on the consumer recognition factor established and enjoyed by the franchise.

Franchisees also tend to capitalize on commonality in "back office" operations. Activities such as accounting, training, recruiting, client contact and strategic planning tend to be similar if not identical within the members of a specific franchise. The rationale behind the similarity is quite simple. Franchisees rely on the franchisor to provide them with systems and methods that have met the test of experience and been found to be the most efficient and effective available. After all, part of what a firm is paying for in a franchise is guidance and direction on how to run a profitable operation.

Owners of independent firms are also anxious to emulate proven success patterns, but they tend to think that they can improve on most of them by adding a particular nuance peculiar to their firm and its marketplace and/or by injecting into the formula their personal creativity and inventiveness. In some quarters, such an attitude is seen as an overabundance of egoism, certainly a trait somewhat characteristic of owners of independent real estate firms. Others, however, identify the independents' approach as classically entrepreneurial, the stuff that Horatio Alger success stories are built on.

One attribute of success in the real estate field—found regularly in both franchisees and independent operators—is the ability to adapt to changing circumstances. The most successful real estate firms are those that either anticipate the effects of change or respond to them with immediacy and aggressiveness. The mid-to-late-1990s certainly afforded bountiful opportunity for this attribute to be demonstrated.

Changes in communication, changes in consumer sophistication, changes in agency law, changes in licensing standards, changes in technology, changes in the demographics of sales agents, changes in financing methods, changes in organizations representing the real estate profession and, most certainly, changes in the competitive environment punctuated the real estate industry with the aggressiveness of boldface exclamation marks.

Leaders of the industry responded, with activities designed to take advantage of the opportunities afforded by the changes, to offset the problems beset by them and to structure any future industry alterations to their advantage.

THE REALTY ALLIANCE

One such notable activity was the formation of the Realty Alliance, a grouping of some 51 top megabrokers formed by the merger of the Masterminds and the Dozen, two somewhat loosely aligned megabroker "brainstormer" groups. Included in the new organization are 16 of the 25 top-ranked independent firms in the nation in terms of transactional activity.

Prior to forming the Realty Alliance, the Dozen and the Masterminds were quite similar in their activities, meeting periodically in the city of one of their members, spending two or three days thoroughly analyzing the operations of the host member, rendering a comprehensive critique to top management of that firm and spending a number of hours freely sharing information pertaining to key elements of their own business enterprises. From such meetings came numerous ideas in the realm of marketing, recruiting, expansion, mergers, technology, education and, most importantly, routes to profitability.

All such activities were possible without fear of losing competitive advantage and, for the most part, without danger of wandering into antitrust domains, because membership in each organization was limited to one firm per major market. Thus, there were no real estate firms that had membership in both organizations but there were a host of cities that housed one member of each entity.

Each organization wished to confine its membership only to large, multioffice, full-purpose companies that could justifiably be called *megabrokers* and, with very random exception, exclude any organization that, though otherwise qualified, belonged to a franchise.

The aggregate population base of such companies is finite—probably no more than 75 to 100 throughout the nation—and even some of these belonged to lesser-known but similar "networking" organizations, such as the Vision Group. Thus, in the mid-1990s, both the Masterminds and the Dozen found themselves virtually maxed out as far as potential members were conceded. Yet neither thought it had a sufficient critical mass of membership large enough to make the impact on the industry and the contribution to member firms that each desired.

Merger was the answer.

But not without some serious discussions in both groups about the wisdom, workability and wieldiness of such a move.

There was some degree of reluctance, solidly rooted in the fact that many of the firms had been involved in earlier attempts at "corporate togetherness" short of merger, such as the original Amerinet (in the 1980s) or even Previews (in the early 1970s). All such attempts had failed. Most observers attribute their lack of success to the fact that the egos and independence of the involved parties made agreement on key issues virtually impossible.

But both groups dismissed the problem this time, not so much as a result of a change in attitudes on the part of the participants, but rather because of concern about the pace of change and especially about those aspects of change centered around two other entities deeply involved in the real estate industry's present and future, each of which has been examined earlier in this book—the National Association of REALTORS® and HFS.

The Realty Alliance voices no hostility toward the National Association of REALTORS®, yet many of the undertakings and activities in its proposed modus operandi for the near future would find it active in many of the same areas as the NAR. At least some of the Realty Alliance's plans for the future are based on prior concerns among the megabrokers in the Dozen and the Masterminds about what the NAR was and was not doing.

On the activity side, there has been considerable dismay about "organized real estate" attempting to provide for its total membership goods and services in the fields of education, recruiting, technology and group purchasing power that the large brokerage firms were able to provide for themselves. Devotees of organized real estate often refer to this as "leveling the playing field." Megabrokers are opposed to "leveling the playing field" after they have expended considerable time, money and effort to tilt the playing field in their favor.

Nowhere was this problem perceived as being more acute than in the areas of multiple listing services and in the realm of Internet presence.

REFINING SOURCES: THE MLS AND THE INTERNET

The MLS has been a localized, or at most, regionalized, operation. The NAR neither owns, runs or even indirectly supervises any multiple-listing system. A few systems are not even owned by local boards of Realtors. However, the NAR Multiple Listing Policy Committee has been instrumental in recommended the procedures under which many local systems operate. Thus, more than a modicum of critical comment about MLSs seeps through to NAR.

Largely, however, the concern of megabrokers regarding MLS involves jurisdiction and location, pricing and control. The first part of the problem has, for the most part, been rectified by movements toward consolidations of MLSs systems throughout the nation.

Prior to such consolidation, megabrokers often had to belong to a sizable number of individual MLSs in order to properly cover a metropolitan marketplace. In Greater Chicagoland, for example, before the emergence of the Northern Illinois Regional Multiple Listing Service in the early 1990s, companies seeking areawide access to listing inventory had to belong to 16 MLSs, each with its own dues, fees and, quite often, duplication of listings.

Increasingly, the multiplicity of localized multiple-listing services has been replaced by consolidation along metropolitan, regional and, in many cases, even multiregional lines.

Yet the stigma remains, at least to some extent, supporting the notion of organized real estate being an overstaffed bureaucracy.

Pricing is another matter. For many years, a vast majority of local associations of REALTORS® financed (or subsidized) the board, its employees and its various functions from revenue received from MLS dues and fees. As might be expected, large brokerage firms (and some small ones as well) did not appreciate being "overcharged" in MLS fees in order to support other board activities, many of which they had little or no interest in. Due largely to the "board of choice" concept adopted by NAR in the early 1990s, most boards have had to adjust their MLS fees and place formerly subsidized activities on a self-supporting basis.

But, the perception still exists. Many practitioners feel as though organized real estate will take financial advantage of them whenever possible.

The final aspect of megabrokerage concern about the MLS is related closely to the first two. Inequities and indirections in jurisdictions and prices would not exist, the large firms contend, if control of the MLS was in the hands of its dominant users. Instead, they often found situations in which MLS boards, directorates or committees were often controlled by representatives of small brokerage firms. Election to such posts on the basis of "one firm, one vote" gave rise to such a situation.

"Change all of this," said many of the megabrokers in numerous communities throughout the country, "and run the MLS like a business, run the board like a self-sustaining enterprise, adjust MLS fees in relationship to actual costs, and give those firms whose activities actually support the system a dominant role in its governance." "If such changes are not made," they implied—or threatened, "we will withdraw and start our own version of the MLS."

Faced with such firmly stated possibilities, many boards and MLSs made necessary changes and today are more in line with what most observers would consider good business practices.

Yet, the reputation was firmly implanted, and, oddly enough, attached itself not just to local organizations, but to the totality of organized real estate, especially to the NAR.

The NAR caught a fair share of criticism and ill feeling for MLS "abuses" even though it did not run a single MLS.

As mentioned earlier in this book, the NAR's abortive effort to dominate the real estate presence on the Internet through the REALTORS® Information Network (RIN) drew harsh reaction from major segments of the association's member population. The megabrokers who ultimately formed the Realty Alliance were among the most vocal critics and adversaries. To some degree, the Realty Alliance was created to make sure the efforts of "organized real estate" did not tilt the real estate playing field against the regional megabrokers.

As John Moore, president of Genesis Relocation Services and a 25 year veteran in the industry sees it, "I think the RIN as much as anything else was the reason the Realty Alliance happened. There were the Dozen and the Masterminds. They reached the conclusion that together they would have much more clout in directing organizations like the NAR if they were ever to start something like the RIN again or anything else along those lines."

As detailed earlier, Moore was quick to seize an opportunity created by the arrival of The Realty Alliance when he convinced its leadership to coventure with his organization (Genesis) in starting a new relocation service company (Reliance Relocation Service).

RELO, the relocation network with the largest number of independent broker members also has stepped up its member recruiting and promotional efforts since the RIN debacle and the HFS takeover of PHH.

Few, if any, Realty Alliance members would attest to the stimulation given to the organization by the activities of the NAR, preferring instead to focus on the proactive positive features and functions incorporated into the new organization.

They would be reluctant also to admit that another driving force of their merger entity was the need to establish a stronger competitive force against HFS; yet privately, many will freely state that for the past couple of years, since HFS made its initial forays into the world of real estate franchising, their strategic plan has been consistently adjusted to respond to the ever growing forceful presence of the industry giant. To be sure, many of the following activities, listed by the Realty Alliance as "under consideration" as goals of the organization seem to closely parallel HFS:

- Possible startup, purchase, merger or alliance to establish a major national presence in the fields of residential mortgage, referral network, affinity marketing and corporate relocation
- Leveraging of collective purchasing power in numerous areas, including group rates for broadcast and print media
- Effective use of political clout in Washington
- Marketing on the Internet
- Training programs for managers and support personnel
- Development of a "world class" awards convention for top producers

Expectation among its charter members is that the Realty Alliance will have the ability to expand and will find the capital to fund both membership growth and needed products, programs and services required by members—and, perchance, to compete effectively with HFS.

INDEPENDENTS AND FRANCHISES COPE

Strong independents outside the Realty Alliance also are structuring themselves to deal with the eccentricities of change and the challenges of new competition. Many are attempting to solidify and expand their market presence, often by employing on a local or regional level virtually the same tactics that HFS is using on the national scene. Rampant mergers between independent firms continue, generally followed by consolidation of overlapping offices and operational redundancies. Many brokerage firms have established their own localized affinity relationships with various corporate and institutional organizations and have established vendor alliances with a host of local merchants.

Those franchise organizations not controlled by HFS are closely following that conglomerate's movements as they plot their own plans for the future. Actually, beyond the scope of the Century 21-ERA-Coldwell Banker triumvirate within the HFS family, there is no superfluity of national franchises. Probably only three truly merit the title of "national." They are Prudential Real Estate Affiliates (PREA), Better Homes and Gardens Realty Services (BH&G) and RE/MAX International. Realty Executives would be considered a fourth strong contender in parts of the nation but simply does not have enough universal coverage to join the "nationals." Still another one-time contender, Realty World, apparently has abandoned the field of franchising.

Realty World

Realty World was a major factor in the field for the first of its two decades of existence but one that has steadily declined in membership and marketshare over the past ten years, Early in 1997, it embarked upon a course of action shifting from a franchise to a "marketing network" called Realty World Broker Network. It targeted small brokerage firms desiring national name recognition and affiliation and the ability to obtain goods and services without the restrictions and costs inherent in a franchise. A broker-owner could join the "Network" for a one-time fee of $2,500, then pay monthly dues of $250 (plus $150 per month for each associate). The initial membership period was five years, although either party to the agreement could opt out after six months. Renewal after the five-year period was $250. For those sums a member had supposedly access to state-of-the-art tools and marketing systems, an international member-to-member referral service, training and support systems and access to affiliations, strategic alliances and group purchasing power. Existing Realty World franchisees were being encouraged to convert to the Network organization but could continue as franchisees until the termination date of their contract.

As of midsummer 1997, however, this thrust into a Broker Network Concept was discarded, at least temporarily. Realty World underwent another of its frequent changes in ownership and reportedly has yet to determine precisely what its new "modus operandi" might be. New Realty World ownership also has a vested interest in other small franchise entities, including Homelife, which though quite minimally present in the United States, is well represented in Canada, its country of origin.

Meanwhile, the three non-HFS giants of the real estate franchise field are busily engaged in pursuing their own strategic goals and tactical maneuvers.

Prudential Real Estate Affiliates (PREA)

Defying rumors that have been rampant for the past several years, Prudential Insurance Company of America seems committed to the continued support and growth of its real estate franchise subsidiary. In fact, knowledgeable observers suggest that PREA will either have its own version of a "buying entity" somewhat similar to NRT Inc. or it will receive a substantial cash infusion from its parent company to use in acquiring major independents and converting them to franchises, and to serve as a "buyout" fund available, if needed, to acquire superlarge PREA franchises. Most of the owners of the large PREA franchises came into the system when Prudential acquired Merrill Lynch Realty several years ago, then converted all Merrill Lynch company-owned facilities to licensed franchises, with former Merrill Lynch regional directors assuming ownership in most instances. Prudential evidenced its new expansion vigor during the summer of 1997 when, in short order, it assisted top southern California franchisee, Pacific California Realty/San Diego, in acquiring the Ellis Realty Group, a ten-office company with 350 sales associates in Orange and San Diego Counties, and then stimulating of northern California megabroker Mason McDuffie and its $1 billion annual sales volume, to affiliate with PREA under the Prudential California Realty franchise.

In addition, Prudential Insurance has embarked on a corporatewide effort called the "One Prudential Initiative." This multifaceted campaign blends together public identification of the various Prudential divisions, such as insurance, securities and real estate. Part of the plan calls for several of Prudential's consumer-oriented activities to be housed together in activity centers under one roof. At the start, insurance agents will be housed in certain real estate brokerage centers. Three test-market sites for such an undertaking have been opened—in Minneapolis, Minnesota, Richmond, Virginia and Phoenix, Arizona. The company goal is to have 100 of these "co-locations" functioning by early 1998. In 1996, PREA on its own attempted a somewhat similar endeavor, testing a "Home Center" concept structured to help home-seeking consumers in free-standing facilities thoroughly equipped with modern computer technology but absent the presence of sales agents. It was abandoned after a single store, one-year trial run in West Hartford, Connecticut. The new endeavor seems to have a much broader potential impact, as it extends recognition of the Prudential name from one divisional activity to another.

In a major attempt to differentiate itself from its competition, PREA continues to vigorously promote its "Value Range Marketing" program, a system where properties are listed for sale within a price spread rather than at a precise figure. The program has its strong supporters and its detractors, both within and outside the Prudential network. Top PREA officials admit it is "not for everyone" but contend that in many sectors of the nation, properties listed under the program have sold much more quickly than comparable "fixed-price" listings (64 percent of the Valve Range Marketing properties sell in less than two months, according to company officials). Reportedly, 65 percent of the properties listed under the "Value Range Marketing" plan sell above the median range of the suggested prices.

The current leadership team at Prudential came into place in September 1996. It is headed by Steven Ozonian, who advanced into the president and CEO post following a sudden and abrupt resignation of former top executive Steve Bauer. Ozonian had held the posts of senior executive vice president and COO. John Van Der Wahl, former senior counsel for the Prudential Diversified Group (to which PREA reports) replaced Ozonian as COO.

Better Homes and Gardens Realty Services (BH&G)

Both PREA and BH&G have been focusing their recruiting concentration on the acquisition of megabrokers into their networks. Often, the direct costs incurred by a franchisor in recruiting new members is substantial—both in terms of "conversion costs allowances" and other financial incentives extended by the franchisor to the new franchisee and with respect to operational considerations. Regarding the latter, for example, under certain circumstances, BH&G no longer requires its larger franchisees to use the standard franchise signage package. It also encourages its dominant franchisees to offset their franchise fees by establishing a sort of sub-network within their metropolitan areas, recruiting smaller brokerage firms to the franchise and then functioning as a centralized serving source for the smaller entities. PREA has a somewhat similar area development program, especially active in California where a sizable number of relatively small firms belong to PREA through an "umbrella" relationship with megafranchise Prudential of California.

In mid-1997, BH&G announced its plans to follow what it considers to be a "contrarian" strategy in its approach to its franchisees vis-à-vis other networks. In a move described by CEO Sabbag as "swimming against the stream," BH&G is committing itself to an intensification of its member services, with additional field personnel maintaining more direct contacts with member firms and their agents. A central facet of this commitment is the plan for on-site delivery in member offices of more than 300 training classes, specifically customized for BH&G franchisees. Sabbag notes that his organization is adding field personnel and member services at a time when a number of other franchises are reducing the size of their field and member service staffs.

RE/MAX

Prudential Real Estate Affiliates, Better Homes and Gardens and the three HFS franchise brands all fall into a category generally described as "traditional real estate franchises." By contrast, RE/MAX is usually looked upon as extremely nontraditional.

It has ever been such, perhaps even more so in its early days.

In the late 1970s and early 1980s, as RE/MAX established itself as a national participant on the real estate scene, most of the other entrants in the field regarded it as synonymous with "the 100 percent concept." Many also regarded the notion of awarding a sales agent 100 percent of a commission (after collecting a monthly administrative or "desk" fee) as a passing fancy destined to collapse rather faster than it was launched. They thought a franchise structured on such an arrangement to be a foolhardy endeavor.

They were wrong on all counts.

RE/MAX has not only grown and prospered, it also has reset the operational mode for most of its competitors along the way.

After initially scoffing at the idea of a 100 percent commission concept, brokers throughout the nation were soon cursing the effectiveness of the notion as they witnessed many of their top level sales agents departing their ranks to transfer to a RE/MAX office where they could receive what they perceived to be "their fair share" of compensation, and, in effect, "run their own show" in an environment devoid of newcomers and subpar agents.

To protect their own most valuable asset—productive agents—RE/MAX competitors quickly adopted their own version of the "100 percent concept"—or some slight modification thereof. A sizable number did so as an option open to successful agents. Those who continued to reject the notion of the "100 percent concept" nonetheless needed to protect their agents from transferring to RE/MAX. For the most part, they did so by altering commission structures, often increasing the share paid to agents to 60 percent, 70 percent, 80 percent and even higher—all while continuing to offer and pay for support services and mechanisms which, in the RE/MAX system, are absorbed by the agents themselves.

The net result for the industry as a whole has been to elevate the importance of successful agents and to tilt the financial rewards in their direction and away from the brokerage firm and its proprietors. Thus, RE/MAX has long been regarded by many competitors as a major cause for the decline in general industry profitability. As one well known independent owner put it, "RE/MAX has taken all the fun and profit out of real estate."

To be sure, many leading firms have adjusted to the situation and have realigned their profit picture upward—largely by assessing, directly or indirectly, various charges to the agents that previously were handled by the firm. Some firms might also develop a sizable segment of "company-generated" business, which they then assign to agents—at a substantially reduced commission split. But many are those who did not recover and saw red ink splash vividly across their income statements, in many cases resulting in their merger or sale to another firm or to their outright liquidation.

Both those who remain and those who departed today freely admit that RE/MAX reconfigured the playing field.

Today, RE/MAX is no longer considered an aberration on the real estate scene. Its growth has been without interruption as far as agents (now in excess of 47,000) and franchised offices (nearly 3,000) are concerned. For the most part, it remains a haven for highly successful agents whose experience and commitment to the industry is evidenced by the fact that, of the 47,000 agents, nearly 18,000 possess a professional designation—38 percent of total RE/MAX franchise population, the highest percentage among national franchises and more than double that of the overall industry average.

RE/MAX remains the only major franchise group whose control is in the hands of the independent entrepreneurs who founded it—Dave Liniger and Gail Liniger—along with a cadre of long tenured and trusted top-echelon executives such as newly named corporate president Daryl Jesperson.

The future of RE/MAX and its input on the industry seems to rest squarely on the shoulders of a small cadre of individuals. Their commitment over the past two decades has been to continued growth and development of the franchise and its members. There seems to be no indication that they are wavering from such ends as the millennium approaches. Yet there comes a time when even the most tireless of innovators and the most ambitious of company builders consider moving on to other facets of human endeavor. One wonders what the future might hold for RE/ MAX should its principals be confronted with such a consideration.

There are no such signs at the moment, however, so it appears likely that for the foreseeable future RE/MAX must be regarded as a major competitive participant in the real estate brokerage arena, continuing to challenge old-line "traditional" methods and methodologies. But, thanks to HFS, it no longer is the only such challenger.

In all, the presence of the Realty Alliance, staunch independents, RE/MAX, Prudential Real Estate Affiliates, Better Homes and Gardens, Realty Executives, and other lesser-known franchises should assure observers that regardless of the impact of any one entrant in the field, the terrain of real estate brokerage activity will remain a vibrantly competitive one for quite some time to come.

CHAPTER 5

Demographics: Your Secret Weapon!

Fact: The United States had about 20.4 million births between January 1990 and December 1994. That was more than in any five-year period since the end of the baby boom (1960 to 1964).

Fact: Only about one-third of U.S. households have any children under the age of 18, while one-fourth contain people who live alone.

Fact: The total purchasing power of the top 20 percent of the U.S. households now equals the middle 60 percent of the population's earnings.

Fact: The median household income of college graduates is $55,000, 76 percent higher than median incomes for all households.

Fact: Nearly 50 percent of the immigrants coming to the United States in the last ten years are 25 to 44 years old and are considered prime home-buying age. More than 800,000 immigrants, particularly Asian and Hispanic, entered the United States in 1996.

Fact: In 1995 one-third of the children in the United States are African American, Hispanic, or Asian.

Fact: Between 1990 and 1995, 52 percent of the growth in the United States occurred in the ten most populous states.

Demographics of the U.S. population will have a significant impact on the residential real estate industry! They will impact the number of homes bought and sold, the prices of homes, the styles and amenities in those homes, home location and much more. Those who know the demographic makeup of their markets will have a distinct advantage over those who do not.

This chapter focuses mostly on national demographic issues that will help you prepare for your future in real estate. There will undoubtedly be some aspects touched upon that do affect you, whether on a national level or on a level that impacts your market.

OLDER MAY BE BETTER?

The age of the home buyer or seller has a significant impact on multiple aspects of the home purchase. A recent study, *The Power of Cohorts,* by Geoffrey Meredith and Charles Schewe, has identified eight different age groups, or cohorts. Each age group has different desires and needs related to the home purchase. Each group also varies in size, which may help in deciding which niches are most appropriate for your needs.

The cohorts range in population from only 4 million in the very senior citizen cohort (age 85 and older) to 69 million in the under 20-year-old cohort. Those under age 20 won't be buying a house from you soon, but many of them will be buying within the next 10 to 15 years—plenty of time to prepare. Most people think the big group is the baby boomers (ages 42 to 50), but they are only about 33 million strong.

A look at Table 5.1 gives some insight on the impact a person's age has on the purchase of a home. The two cohorts aged 75 to 84 and 85 or older are more security minded and interested in familiar surroundings. There won't be much home buying in this group of approximately 17 million people. They will mostly stay where they are or go to some type of organized care facility. The World War II cohort, ages 69 to 74, of about 11 million will be very conservative in their spending. The Post War cohort, ages 51 to 68, will be interested in comfort and security. This 41-million-person cohort also has the cash to spend, so help them enjoy their new surroundings of comfort and security. The two baby boomer cohorts, Boomers I (ages 42 to 50) and Boomers II (ages 31 to 41) have enjoyed economic good times most of their lives and are much more willing to meet their personal needs through home ownership. Many of them have gone to college, which means their disposable income will be considerably more than most of the other age groups. The median household income of college graduates is $55,000, which is 76 percent higher than median incomes for all households. A good market niche to farm would include either baby boomer cohort, because they like to spend and have the money. Watch the resort properties go "through the roof" in cost as the Boomers I cohort, in particular, purchase second homes (for more on this, see the section on resort homes later in this chapter). The Generation X cohort is more self-centered and cynical. This 20- to 30-year-old group comprises first-time home buyers, who seem to find the resources when they are convinced they have found the right house for them. Those with college educations will have personal resources or be assertive in getting what they need to get what they want.

Of course, none of the above conclusions holds true in all cases. Those within a cohort have many commonalties, but

TABLE 5.1 The Impact of Eight Cohorts on Home-Buying Behaviors From 1995 Census Estimates for the U.S. Population

Age	# in Millions	% of Total Population	Cohort	Motives
85+	4	1.5	Pre Depression	Current age impacts need for security, shelter and supportive family.
75–84	13	5	Depression Era	Hard times impact their spending, saving and debt.
69–74	11	4	World War II	Unified by a common enemy and shared experience. They are intensely romantic. Although not a boom time, unemployment is no longer a problem. Conservative spending.
51–68	41	16	Post War	Expectation of good times became engraved in society. Global unrest, threat of nuclear power and cold war drive need for certainty in everyday life. Enjoy feeling of comfort, security, family.

TABLE 5.1 The Impact of Eight Cohorts on Home-Buying Behaviors From 1995 Census Estimates for the U.S. Population

42–50	33	12.5	Boomers I	Major political deaths (e.g., Kennedy and King) signal end of status quo. Have experienced economic good times and want a lifestyle at least as good as the one experienced as children in the 1950s.
31–41	49	19	Boomers II	"Idealistic fervor of youth disappeared." Preoccupied with self. Debt is a means of maintaining a lifestyle.
20–30	41	16	Generation X	"Children of divorce and day care, latch-key kids searching for anchors." Political conservatism motivated by "what's in it for me cynicism."
Under 20	<u>69</u>	<u>26</u>	Good Times Kids	Longest sustained economic prosperity in modern times—they want it all.
Total	261	100.0		

Source: Information modified from *The Power of Cohorts*, by Geoffrey Meredith and Charles Schewe, published by American Demographics in December 1994.

like properties, each person is unique and different. Use the
above information and Table 5.1 to help you make decisions
on who to market to and how to interact with those in each
cohort. If you choose to niche market a cohort, learn as
much additional information as you can about their special
needs.

THE AGING OF SOCIETY

As we move from now to the year 2010, the population in
general will be aging. The over-65 group will increase from
33.5 million in 1995 to 40 million by the year 2010. Interest-
ingly enough, the actual percentage of the general population 65 and older will not change. The U.S. Census Data
suggests that this group will continue to account for about
13 percent of the U.S. population from now to the year
2010 (see Table 5.2).

The age group that both increases in size and in percentage is the 45- to 64-year-old group. We see an increase from
51.5 million or about 20 percent of the general population,
to 79 million, or slightly over 26 percent of the general population. The final two home-buying age groups, ages 25 to
34 and 35 to 44, decrease slightly in numbers and in percentage of the total population during this time. They both
decrease in number from 42 million, or 16 percent to 38
and 40 million, respectively, and about 13 percent of the
population by the year 2010. This is not bad news for the
real estate industry. The ever-growing 45 to 64 year olds
have special needs and can frequently afford to satisfy those
needs. When they are also well educated, look for a knowledgeable approach to buying and selling real estate. This
age group will be demanding more and better quality service from the industry. If we do not give the type and level
of quality service they want, they will search for it and get it
from someone else.

TABLE 5.2 Demographic Information on Ages

	General Population*								
	25–34 Years Old		35–44 Years Old		45–64 Years Old		65+ Years Old		
	#†	% of Total	#†	% of Total	#†	% of Total	#†	% of Total	Total
1995	42	16.0	42	16.0	51.5	19.6	33.5	12.7	263
2000	38	13.8	45	16.3	60	21.7	35	12.7	276
2005	37	12.8	43	14.9	70	24.3	37	12.8	288
2010	38	12.7	40	13.3	79	26.3	40	33.3	300

Real Estate Brokers‡

	% of Total	% of Total	% of Total	% of Total
1987	12	26	52	11
1993	6	24	61	10
1996	8	20	62	10

Real Estate Sales Associates‡

	% of Total	% of Total	% of Total	% of Total
1987	23	30	41	6
1993	18	27	48	7
1996	14	26	52	8

*These numbers do no consider people who are younger than 25 years old. Because people under 25 years of age are not included, the numbers do not add up to 100 percent. They are U.S. Census Bureau data estimates.

†Numbers are in millions of people.

‡Source: National Association of REALTORS®.

An interesting dynamic is that the ages of real estate brokers and sales associates are very different than the ages of the general population. Whereas only about 20 percent of the general population in 1995 is 45 to 64 years old, 62 percent of the brokers and 52 percent of the sales associates are that age. The 45- to 64-year-old group of real estate professionals has been increasing in size, as has the general population. Brokers may want to think about who they recruit in the future. It may be appropriate to have an office that more closely represents the age of the general population. At the least, brokers may want to consider having an office that more clearly mirrors their local market or market needs.

WHO WILL BE THE MAJORITY BY 2010?

Despite all the predictions that African Americans, Hispanics, and Asians will have a significantly increasing presence in the country, U.S. Census Bureau statistics suggest this is not going to be the situation (see Table 5.3). African Americans ages 25 to 34 are the same in number, while those ages 35 to 44 will increase in numbers but only slightly. There is an increase of African Americans ages 45 to 64 and 65 and over. Those ages 45 to 64 increase from 5.25 million in 1995 to 9.0 million by 2010. Those ages 65 and older increase in number from 2.75 million in 1995 to 3.5 million in 2010. Since African Americans live more evenly throughout the United States than do other minorities, the increase in their members will not seem that dramatic. For example, although African Americans ages 45 to 64 increase in number from 5.25 million to 9 million from 1995 to 2010, whites in the same age range increase from 41 million to 58.5 million during the same time period. In addition, African Americans age 65+ increase in number from 2.75 million to 3.5 million from 1995 to 2010. Whites

TABLE 5.3   Age of General Population* and Various Types of Citizenry

	25–34 Years Old		35–44 Years Old		45–64 Years Old		65+ Years Old		Total
	#†	% of Total	#†	% of Total	#†	% of Total	#†	% of Total	
General Population*									
1995	42	16	42	16	15.5	20	33.5	13	263
2000	38	14	45	16	60.0	22	35.0	13	276
2005	37	13	43	15	70.0	24	37.0	13	288
2010	38	13	40	13	79.0	26	40.0	13	300
White (Not Hispanic)									
1995	29.50	11.0	31.50	12.0	41.0	15.5	28.75	11.0	
2000	25.75	9.3	32.75	11.9	46.5	16.8	29.50	10.7	
2005	24.00	8.3	30.00	10.4	53.5	18.6	30.25	10.1	
2010	24.50	8.2	26.25	8.8	58.5	19.5	32.25	10.8	
African American									
1995	5.50	2.0	5.00	2.0	5.25	2.0	2.75	1.1	
2000	5.25	1.9	5.50	2.0	6.25	2.2	3.00	1.0	
2005	5.25	1.8	5.50	1.9	7.75	2.7	3.00	1.0	
2010	5.50	1.8	5.25	1.7	9.00	3.0	3.50	1.2	
Hispanics									
1995	5.00	2.0	4.0	1.5	3.75	1.5	1.5	0.5	
2000	5.25	1.9	5.0	1.8	4.75	1.7	2.0	0.7	
2005	5.25	1.8	5.5	1.9	6.25	2.2	2.5	0.9	
2010	5.75	1.9	5.5	1.8	7.75	2.6	3.0	1.0	

*These numbers do no consider people who are younger than 25 years old. Because people under 25 years of age are not included, the numbers do not add up to 100 percent. They are U.S. Census Bureau data estimates.

† Numbers are in millions of people.

‡ Source: National Association of REALTORS®.

ages 65+ increase in number from 28.75 million to 32.25 million during the same years. The top three states where African Americans reside (New York, California and Texas) are home to only 24 percent of all African Americans. A majority of Hispanics and Asians live in only three states, as we will shortly see.

Hispanics are also increasing in number, but it is predicted they will be about the same proportion of the general population in the year 2010 as they are now. The number of Hispanics in the United States increased from 22 million in 1990 to 26 million in 1995, but this increase is no different than the increase in the general population during those years. Where you live will have an impact on whether you believe this statement. Some 61 percent of all Hispanics living in the United States call one of three states their home: Florida, Texas or California. If you live in one of those three states, you are seeing a proportional increase in Hispanics. There is a larger percentage of Hispanics in the 45 to 64 and 65 and over age groups, but this increase is still relatively small compared to the overall general population (see Table 5.3). In percentage terms, Hispanics age 45 to 64 increase over 100 percent between 1995 and 2010, while Hispanics 65+ increase in population 100 percent. In absolute terms these increases are 4 million and 1.5 million respectively. With the general population increasing 37 million between 1995 and 2010, the 4 million and 1.5 million increases are relatively small. Again, while the rest of the country experiences little shift from a white to an Hispanic population, if you live in California, Texas or Florida the proportionate and absolute population increases will seem and will be much larger compared to the rest of the population, assuming migration patterns stay the same (Hispanics stay in these states and don't move to other states).

A majority of Asians also live in three states: California, New York and Hawaii. Specific U.S. Census Bureau data on Asians could not be identified, but general U.S. Data Statistics show that 56 percent of Asians reside in these three states.

Minorities in general have grown from 1 in 5 U.S. residents in 1980 to 1 in 4 U.S. residents in 1995. Much of that growth seems to have occurred in the 1980s. In 1995 about one-third of all children (ages 0 to 18) in the United States were African American, Hispanic, or Asian. The largest proportion of increase for these minorities is in the childhood years. As these children grow into the buying ages, their buying needs will start to have an impact on buying and selling behaviors. They are a sizable group.

These demographics have a significant impact on the real estate industry. Data were not available to determine the proportion of real estate licensees who are White, African Americans, Hispanic, or Asian. It makes sense that as minorities increase in numbers, whether or not they are increasing in their proportion to all U.S. residents, that brokers recruit and train more and more minorities. This will most probably be in the broker's and the industry's best interest, because people usually like to associate with and buy homes from people most similar to themselves. If the number of minority brokers and agents does not increase, these minority groups may be motivated to use an alternative other than the human real estate professional when buying or selling a home. Technology is gender and race neutral, while the professional assisting in the transaction is not. These groups may be more motivated to use new technologies to displace the human element in the transaction if they do not feel that the human understands and will meet their needs.

MIGRATION AND IMMIGRATION TRENDS—WHERE WILL WE BE TOMORROW?

Schlott states, "The marketplace in America is vast. There are 265 million people. We lose sight of the fact that things are different in Tulsa, Oklahoma, than they are in Houston, Texas, than they are in San Diego, California. So when we make our statements about the industry, a lot of these changes are going to move in unusual ways."

American population trends in 1995 have resulted in some geographic areas with increases, while other geographic areas have had population decreases. Ten states are the home to 54 percent of all U.S. residents. From 1990 to 1995, 52 percent of all the growth in the country was also in those same states.

Although New York was the most populous state in 1950, it is now number 3, having recently been replaced as number 2 by Texas. California, of course, is the most populous state even though it has seen a net migration loss of 1.1 million people between 1990 and 1995. During that same time, New York saw a net migration loss of 1 million people. More than 550,000 have left New England. Connecticut and Rhode Island were two states with significant net decreases in population. In fact, every state in the Northeast had a net migration loss in population between 1990 and 1995.

The states that were the greatest beneficiaries of the migration from 1990 to 1995 were Florida (net influx of 640,000 people), Texas (net influx of 165,000 people) and eight of the ten Rocky Mountain and Northwest states.

The United States had over 20 million births between 1990 and 1995. This was more than in any five-year period since the end of the baby boom (1960 to 1964) and was 6 percent more than in the late 1980s. If good economic times persist, this trend will probably continue between now and the year 2000. Natural increases (births minus deaths) accounted for about two-thirds of the population growth in the United States from 1990 to 1995. The other one-third came from immigration. From 1990 to 1995, 4.6 million immigrants entered the country. This was the highest total this century and more than 30 percent increase over the 1985 to 1989 five-year period. There currently is a backlash about the number of people immigrating to the United States each year, with talk about passing laws to decrease immigration. The outcome will depend on whether any legislation is passed as well as how that legislation is implemented.

From 1990 to 1995, approximately 200,000 to 300,000 illegal immigrants entered the United States. This is 9 to 12 percent of the entire population growth during that time. Estimates suggest that illegal immigrants live primarily in California (40 percent), New York (15 percent), Florida (11 percent) and Texas (10 percent). Another 10 percent live in Illinois, New Jersey, and Arizona. It is estimated that 86 percent of the illegal immigrants live in these seven states; and the remaining 14 percent live in the other 43 states. Of the more than 4 million people who moved to the United States from 1990 to 1995, more than 50 percent of them moved into California, Florida or Texas. These three states accounted for 37 percent of all U.S. growth during these five years, even considering the 1.1 million–person out-migration from California.

The economic impact of illegal aliens may or may not be significant. It is estimated that $3.1 billion is spent in these seven states to educate the illegal immigrants. Another $445 million is spent on Medicare. Prison costs account for an additional $470 million. On the positive side, it is estimated these illegal aliens pay $1.9 billion in direct taxes and account for billions more spent on consumer items.

Immigrants, both legal and illegal, can be a positive force in home sales. "Immigrants place a high premium on home ownership, and they are more willing to make sacrifices to buy," states John Tuccillo, Chief Economist for the National Association of REALTORS®. According to a Fannie Mae report,

"Eight in ten immigrants believe that owning a home symbolizes their integration into American life. Immigrants who rent are nearly three times as likely as all adult renters to consider home buying their number one priority." In addition, Michael Lee, president of Seminars Unlimited, states that "REALTORS® tend to be more reluctant to work with immigrants than immigrants are to work with REALTORS®." He also suggests that Hispanics have a culture that supports extended families. This means that when they are in the market to buy a home they are looking for something bigger than what may be otherwise suspected.

Immigrants are a new market area to tap. To date it seems that real estate professionals may be reluctant to effectively market to this new niche. As more and more immigrants enter the home buying arena this seems to be a place where both brokers and sales agents can establish new and expanding markets and relationships. Those living in California, Texas and Florida in particular therefore need to keep in mind the increasing presence of minorities and immigrants in these three states.

BABY BOOMERS AND OTHER TRENDS

According to John Tuccillo, "Every 7½ seconds someone in the United States turns 50 years old. This will keep happening for the next 15 years." It seems there are quite a few baby boomers, and their home-buying needs and habits will have a significant impact on home purchases in the future. Add the Post War cohort to the baby boomer groups and we have a very significant home-buying force. We have already seen that there are 33 million of Boomers I, ages 42 to 50; 49 million of Boomers II, ages 31 to 41; and 41 million in the Post War cohort, ages 51 to 68. All of these people are of home-buying age. Many of them have considerable resources to purchase one or more homes. 123 million people can buy a lot of real estate. The questions are *will* they buy, and if so, what *will* they buy?

There are many theories on what these 123 million will purchase. It has been suggested that the post war generation (ages 51 to 68) will be most interested in smaller carefree homes. Or perhaps they will be looking for only as much home as they need, including low maintenance but plenty of amenities. The migration of this group will be to the sun and/or to the mountains.

The two baby boomer cohorts (ages 42 to 50 and 31 to 41) will be most interested in homes that meet the needs of their families. But what warrants a family? The latest statistics show that only about one-third of households have children under 18. Nearly one-fourth of households are people living alone. Women who live alone form 15 percent of all U.S. households, and many of them are widows. Single men who live alone form about 10 percent of all households, and most of them are less than 45 years of age. Households earning $50,000 or more consist of a married couple 80 percent of the time. Households earning $100,000 or more consist of a married couple 86 percent of the time.

The year-2000 definition of a family appears to be much different than the traditional two adults and, on average, two children of yesteryear. Dual-career families seem to be the ones with the greatest consumption of goods and services. These will, in many cases, be the niche to market to, assuming you can find them. Chapter 6 provides additional discussion of family composition, mobility, jobs and location.

The education level of the home buyer and seller also has a tremendous impact on the real estate professional. This impact occurs in two ways. First, it effects the earning capacity of the consumer. College graduates are heads of households 68 percent of the time when there is $100,000 or more in earnings. The median household income of all college graduates is $55,000, 76 percent higher than the median income for all households. The total purchasing power of the top 20 percent of United States households, many of which have one or two college graduates at the head, now equals the middle 60 percent of the population's earnings. A college education typically means more disposable income for the purchase of a home.

The second way education will impact the real estate professional in the future is related to the consumers' knowledge of the home transaction and their willingness to use technology in this transaction. The more-educated consumer will be more motivated to use electronic media throughout the entire home purchase transaction. Real estate professionals will best serve themselves if they include electronic media in the presentation, communication and other issues of their relationship with the increasingly affluent college graduate.

The Abelson Trends Report™ suggests four other trends will increase and will have an impact on the home purchase itself. First, health care needs will lead to different home and community designs (up from economic and legal trend #13 in 1995 to economic and legal trend #4 in the year 2000).

Second, first-time buyers will get a tax deduction (up from economic and legal trend #18 in 1995 to economic and legal trend #11 in the year 2000).

Third, the percent of those renting instead of purchasing homes will increase (up from economic and legal trend #16 in 1995 to economic and legal trend #10 in the year 2000).

Fourth, more professionals will work at home, leading to the need for larger homes (up from economic and legal trend #12 in 1995 to economic and legal trend #7 in the year 2000).

Each of these trends should be considered when developing market niches and deciding who to work with in the future.

In summary, college-educated, dual-career families have the resources to invest in real estate. Health care needs, a tax deduction for first-time buyers and larger homes when homes are the choice over rentals will also affect home buying choices. Look to work with consumers in the Boomers I or Post War cohorts. They will be in their prime earning years, and their interests may include investing and/or owning real estate. At the least, be aware that the top 20 percent of the socioeconomic ladder are the ones with money to spend on housing.

HOME OWNERSHIP—VALUE AND PRICE

Home ownership is valued in our society. The general population owns their homes. Those who are 30 to 34 years of age own their home 52 percent of the time. People 70 to 74 years of age own their home about 80 percent of the time. These statistics have remained almost unchanged during the 1990s.

This large proportion of home ownership has continued even as the median price of homes has increased over the last several years. In January 1997 the median price for a home was $120,500; in January 1996 it was $118,000; and in January 1995 it was $112,900. In 1995 there were 3.94 million home units sold, while in 1996 there were 4.085 million units sold. Despite the rising price, there remains a demand to obtain the "American dream" of home ownership.

There are differences in regions regarding home sales and home prices, and some of these are rather drastic. For example, the West continues to be the most expensive area of the country to live. In 1996 830,000 resales occurred at a median cost of $156,000. The South saw the most homes sold (1,450,000) but also had the lowest median price ($103,500). The Midwest had 1,000,000 homes sold, while the Northeast saw 590,000 homes sold at a median price of $141,500.

1996 was a very good year for real estate, with both 4.085 million home units resold and a median price of $120,500—being all-time records.

TOP REAL ESTATE MARKETS NOW AND IN THE NEAR FUTURE

Valuation International, Ltd., of Atlanta, surveys 45 major markets in the United States on an annual basis. Taking a closer look at several of the factors they examine will give insight into the hottest markets in the country now and in the near future. Table 5.4 shows the cities that ranked in the top ten in 1995 for each of the six factors we chose to include. These six factors are 1) percentage change, 2) absolute change, 3) population change, 4) household growth, 5) household income growth, and 6) employment growth (see Table 5.4). The table also shows how the cities will rank on the same factors in the year 2000. There are 20 cities in all ranked because each city appeared at least once in the top ten for one of the six factors in 1995 or the year 2000.

We have added some data to the information supplied by Valuation International Ltd. First, we have counted the number of times a particular city was ranked in the top ten for 1990 to 1995 and the top ten for 1995 to 2000. Second, we counted the number of times that a city moved from not being in the top ten in 1995 to being in the top ten by the year 2000. Third, we ranked the top three cities according to the number of times that city was ranked in the top ten. We did this for both the 1990 to 1995 time period and the 1995 to 2000 time period. The number adjacent to each city is where that city ranked. "1" is the highest ranking in that criteria. In situations where two cities tied, the next rank is skipped. For example, if two cities tied with a rank of #1,

TABLE 5.4 Top 10 Growth Areas

City	Percentage Change† 1990–1995	Percentage Change† 1995–2000	Absolute Change 1990–1995	Absolute Change 1995–2000	Population Change 1990–1995	Population Change 1995–2000	House Growth 1990–1995	House Growth 1995–2000
Atlanta, GA	6	5	7	1	2	6	2	6
Atlantic City, NJ								
Chicago, IL			4	5				
Columbia, SC								
Dallas, TX			1	8	7	9	7	9
Denver, CO								
Fort Worth, TX		6			9	10	8	10
Hartford, CT								
Houston, TX	9	10	2	4	10	8		8
Las Vegas, NV	4	4			1	3	1	3
Los Angeles, CA				6				
Minneapolis, MN			3	9				
Miami, FL								
Nassau-Suffolk, NY								
Orange County, CA		7		3				
Orlando, FL	2	1		10	4	4	5	4
Phoenix, AZ	7	2	9	7	5	1	4	1
San Diego, CA		3		2		5		5
Seattle, WA		8				7		7
West Palm Beach, FL	8	9			3	2	3	2

*Data modified from an article in *Mortgage Banking,* July 1995.

†Numbers below are where this city ranked in the top ten list mentioned in the article from *Mortgage Banking.*

TABLE 5.4 Top 10 Growth Areas (Continued)

City	Household Income Growth		Employment Growth		Times Included in the Six Top 10 Lists		Most Often Change	Ranking of Most Often Listed in a Top 10 List 1990–1995	Ranking of Most Often Listed in a Top 10 List 1995–2000
	1990–1995	1995–2000	1990–1995	1995–2000	1990–1995	1995–2000			
Atlanta, GA			2	9	5	5		1T‡	3T
Atlantic City, NJ		9			0	1			
Chicago, IL					1	1			
Columbia, SC				8	0	1			
Dallas, TX			6	10	4	4			
Denver, CO	8	10			1	1		3T	
Fort Worth, TX		3			2	4			
Hartford, CT	3	2			1	1			
Houston, TX					4	4		3T	
Las Vegas, NV			1	6	4	4		3T	
Los Angeles, CA		7			0	2			
Minneapolis, MN					1	1			
Miami, FL		1			0	1			
Nassau-Suffolk, NY		8			0	1			
Orange County, CA		4		1	0	5	2		3T
Orlando, FL		6	3	3	4	6		3T	1T
Phoenix, AZ			4	2	5	5		1T	3T
San Diego, CA		5		5	0	6	1		1T
Seattle, WA				7	0	4	3		
West Palm Beach, FL				4	3	4			

‡ T = Tied

then the next city, the one with the third highest rank, is ranked #3.

See Table 5.4 for all the information. Some important highlights follow:

- Atlanta is most often listed on a top ten list for the 1990 to 1995 time period. Part of that may have occurred because it was preparing for the 1996 Olympics.
- Orlando and San Diego tied for the hottest marketplace between now and the year 2000. Both cities were listed in the top ten for each of the six factors.
- Atlanta was listed number three as a year 2000 top ten growth market.
- Orlando was the third most frequently listed top ten growth market in 1995. It was listed four times for the 1990 to 1995 time period.
- San Diego was not listed as a 1990 to 1995 top ten city on any of the six factors even though it is estimated to become the number one hottest market in the year 2000. Orange County and Seattle increased the second and third most number of times on top ten lists from the 1990 to 1995 time period to the 1995 to 2000 time period.
- Phoenix was tied with Atlanta as the most often mentioned top ten market in 1995, with five factors ranked in the top ten. By the year 2000, Phoenix is estimated to be listed on five top ten lists again. This puts Phoenix in a tie for third with Orange County and Atlanta as a year 2000 hottest market.
- Dallas, Houston and Las Vegas were listed on four of the six top ten markets for 1990 to 1995, tying them with Orlando for third during that time period.
- California, Texas and Florida had the most cities included on top ten lists. Of the 20 cities appearing on any list, each of these states had three cities listed. California had Los Angeles, Orange County and San Diego. Texas had Dallas, Fort Worth and Houston. Florida had Miami, Orlando and West Palm Beach.

- The South had eight cities on a list, the West had seven cities on a list, the Northeast had three cities on a list, and the Midwest has two cities on a list.
- The cities that had the most significant change from not being listed on a top ten list in 1995 to being listed on a top ten list for the year 2000 were all West Coast cities. San Diego saw the most change in being included, Orange County was second, and Seattle was third.

In summary, there are a number of hot markets projected for the 1995 to 2000 time period. Texas and Florida will remain in vogue, being net gain population states from 1990 to 1995. Texas is predicted to continue its relatively large net influx of people, at least to the year 2000. California is predicted to see a resurgence from its growth years of the 1960s to late 1980s. Time will tell the accuracy of these predictions.

SPECIALTY PROPERTIES—CONDOS AND RECREATIONAL

The number of condominium units sold has increased from 401,000 in 1993 to approximately 475,000 in 1996. This steady growth has been accompanied by a steady increase in per-unit average cost of $83,500 in 1993 to $92,500 in 1996.

Costs and units sold vary per region of the country. The Midwest has seen a steady increase in both sales and prices—the price of one of its 73,000 units sold in 1993 averaged $76,400. By 1996, one of its 84,000 units sold cost $97,200. The South saw a similar increase, with one of its 131,000 units sold in 1993 costing an average of $69,000. By 1996 one of its 156,000 units cost an average of $72,600. The West and Northeast have seen a somewhat more sporadic growth. Condos in the West have fluctuated in the

111,000 to 131,000 unit range per year since 1993. 1996 had about 126,000 units sold at an average price of about $111,000. The Northeast has fluctuated from 86,000 units in 1993 to about 110,000 units in 1996 with an average price in 1996 of about $96,000.

The recreation homes market will continue to see increased sales as we reach the year 2000 and beyond. A Roper Organization study found that in the early 1990s, for the first time, more people said leisure time was more important than working—41 percent preferred leisure, while 36 percent preferred work. In addition, a study by MediaMark Research reported that only 3.5 percent of people in the age group of 35 to 44 years old own a second home while 6.9 percent of people in the age group of 55 to 64 years old own a second home. As the 33 million people in the 42 to 50 year old Boomers I cohort, the 49 million people in the 31 to 41 year old Boomers II cohort, and the 41 million in the 51 to 68 year old Post War cohort act on their leisure needs, the recreational market will become a hotbed of activity. Expect in the next decade a demand for millions of recreational homes (about 5 million). With about 3.8 to 4.1 million homes of all kinds changing hands each year, the recreational market will have a significant impact on the entire home sales market. It seems that record home-sales years will be continuing, assuming no major changes in the economy.

WHAT THE FUTURE HOLDS

"People are going to live where they want to. There is going to probably be less movement. There will truly be virtual communities,"comments Karun Khanna, of US Web Systems.

Expect the virtual community to happen as we progress as a society into varying levels of the electronic era. Add to the increasing electronic era that people are more interested in leisure than work, that there will be more efficient communications via multiple and increasingly rapid electronic media, and that personal resources allow people to purchase homes and to live wherever they want.

Keep in mind, however, that people will have to first move to where they want to be. Also keep in mind that the number of people in the United States is increasing from about 265 million in 1996 to 300 million in 2010. Furthermore, there will be more people owning second homes and many more single heads of households meaning more homes per million people. The bottom line? Barring any economic catastrophe, *real estate sales have nowhere to go but up.*

Some final comments to keep in mind. The market in the near future will see more sales from increasing numbers of immigrants who are motivated to buy homes moreso than is the rest of the population. There will also be a large growth of smaller households who have the resources to purchase what they choose. These purchases may be smaller, but the amenities and the price will be greater. Third, first-time buyers may decrease in number, but second-home purchasers will have a significant and positive impact on the industry. Fourth, the recreational and condo market will expand as the baby boomers get older and look for that ideal second home to get away. Fifth, the electronic media will allow them to work and play anywhere.

The near future looks extremely bright for home sales. The issue is, will the broker and sales associate adjust in time to take advantage of the demography or will some new paradigm to sell real estate beat them at their own game?

CHAPTER 6

Can Consumers Control the Insider Track?

"If you want to accurately predict the real estate activity in any area of the country, look at the job creation figures. If the community is generating jobs, the real estate market will enjoy prosperity. If the jobs are stagnant or declining, the real estate market is likely to head for the doldrums.

John Tuccillo, Consulting Economist to NAR

"The consumer is in the driver's seat."

Such is the refrain of virtually every knowledgeable real estate industry expert as he or she stands on the verge of the 21st century.

But what is the true meaning of such a somewhat well-sounding but nonetheless trite remark?

If, indeed, it means that the real estate business of the future will be comparable to an automobile that responds to the actions and nuances of a person behind the wheel, then some serious analysis of that analogy is in order.

For starters (pun intended), most drivers anticipate putting the key in the ignition, turning it ever so slightly and relying on the vehicle to perform from thereon. Of course, there is a bit of directional navigation on the part of the driver, but technology promises to change even that in the near future with computer guidance systems that automatically route the auto from its point of origination to its destination as voice-directed by the passenger/driver.

Will the consumer of tomorrow demand similar performance from a real estate agent? And, if so, will the agent be able to oblige?

The answer to both these questions is probably yes and no.

Without doubt, homebuyers or homesellers of the near future will want—and expect—their agents to perform a wide variety of tasks connected with disposition or acquisition of their properties. Yet most buyers and sellers probably will continue to want to have a personal involvement in the process other than just saying "I want to buy (or sell) a house."

Most agents, at least the more successful ones, will be able to respond efficiently and effectively to their clients' wants and whims, but it is unlikely they will always be able to consummate a transaction without some considerable involvement on the part of their clients.

Moreover, just as there are some malperforming "clunkers" within the motor vehicle ranks, so too will there be marginal, quasi-functional, and full-scale incompetents among the ranks of licensees. However, with respect to this group, it is unlikely that the automotive analogy will extend to "taking these subpar performers to the repair shop." Rather, they will be dispatched to the junkyard.

Just as the automobile traveler is conscious of time, wanting to reach the terminal point of his or her journey as quickly as possible, so too, on the consumer's "journey" to the destination of new (or former) homeowner, proceeding with dispatch is an important factor. So too is arriving at that destination without the trauma of "traffic jams" and, certainly, without involvement in any accident.

Vehicular problems, congestion, and accidents can be caused by driver error or by operational malfunctioning of the motorcar—so too in the real estate transaction.

On the positive side of the analogy, however, it is quite possible—probably, many observers would say—that the consumer-driven "ride with a Realtor" can be accomplished smoothly and efficiently with no pings and all purrs in the driving apparatus.

After all, the goal of the consumer and the real estate agent is virtually identical. Both want to consummate a transaction as rapidly and as advantageously as possible.

Toward achievement of that mutual goal, the real estate agent has a temporary leg up on the vehicular counterpart. While soothsayers in the art of technology envision the time in the near future when automobiles will be voice-controlled and responsive to the particular inflections and articulations of specific operators, that era has yet to arrive. Fortunately for the real estate industry, it has been in place in relationships between agents and their clients and customers for a long time.

Accomplished real estate practitioners build their reputations and their business success on their ability to attune themselves to the individualized wants and needs, desires and expectations of the consumer. Cloning to the contrary, no two human beings are precisely alike, and no two approaches to satisfying their quests for owning or selling property should be exactly the same.

To maintain the level of achievement that has vaulted them to professional prestige and economic excellence, real estate agents need to continually adjust both to macroscopic changes in society, which affect most individuals, and to those major changes as they affect specific consumers.

Thus, it is of considerable merit to examine both the macrocosm and microcosm of consumers and consumer behavior in the new millennium and the scanty months leading up to it.

SOME GENERALITIES STAND OUT

Relying on such well-regarded popular journals as *American Demographics* and *The Futurist,* the following broad-based generalities about U.S. consumers in the last phases of the 20th and initial years of the 21st centuries can be identified:

- They will have an insistence on quality of product.
- They will demand that quality service accompany both goods and services.
- They will be extremely busy, with a multiplicity of occupational and personal activities demanding their attention. Thus, they will seek "time-saving" goods and services and will assiduously avoid those activities and/ or products that require a personal time commitment on their part.
- For the most part, they will be well educated and sufficiently intelligent to see through any marketing scheme that attempts to substitute promotional veneer or statistical sophistry for hard, cold reality.
- By today's standards, they will be technologically sophisticated, although most will not regard themselves as such because of universal familiarity with technologically based activities previously considered to be just short of wizardry.
- In the aggregate, barring a major cataclysmic event, they will be wealthier than they are today, both in real and inflation-adjusted dollars, although there will continue to be sizable segments of the population in or close to poverty conditions.
- They will be attuned to rapid and continuing change and hence will have less regard for permanence, in goods, lifestyles, cultural standards and even ethical and moral norms.
- Rarely, if ever, will they have the notion of lifetime employment with one employer or even within the confines of one occupational endeavor. Instead, they

will equip themselves with the personal skills adaptable to several career endeavors during the course of a lifetime.

- There will be a recognition and, for the most part, acceptance of widespread diversity along cultural, ethnic, racial, religious and cultural lines. The "melting pot" criteria will apply to matters economic but will not necessarily extend to other facets of life.

To cope with these characteristics of future American consumers, real estate professionals must acquire various attitudinal, occupational and personal approaches to their jobs, some of which might represent radical changes from current methods of operation.

To respond to consumer insistence on quality, agents will have to elevate their personal knowledge and industry sophistication to a new level of expertise. There will be precious little need for the licensee who alternates between accessing multiple-listing information and conducting "drive-by" neighborhood tours and random site inspections. Gone too will be the agents who consider their jobs confined to the tasks of either getting a listing or acquiring an accepted purchase contract, leaving all subsequent and attendant activities connected with the transaction to others.

Disclosure will also be a key qualitative characteristic of successful agents of the future. Full and complete disclosure of any and all aspects of agency relationships, property and neighborhood characteristics and conditions, ancillary activities connected with the transaction and financing opportunities will be minimal consumer expectations. On the other hand, in those situations where an agent is working in the capacity of a disclosed dual agent, with consensual acknowledgment by both parties, there must be rigid adherence to confidentiality in protecting the specific interests and negotiating positions of both buyer and seller. Similarly, in situations involving so-called "designated agency," the commitment to confidentiality imposes a stern obligation upon an entire real estate company.

Consumers of the future will have close to a zero tolerance for deviations from these standards. Instead, they will be keenly aware of the legal approaches they may take to remedy any abridgements from professionalism and the subsequent penalties they might exact from offending real estate agents and firms.

Technology will prove to be the agent's faithful servant and stern taskmaster in responding to future consumer expectations. Its proper and consistent use will enable agents to meet—and even exceed—the time-pressurized deadlines that consumers will expect; however, consumers' increasing familiarity with the capabilities of technology will cause them to be extremely upset and unforgiving of agents who are not at least equally conversant with technology opportunities.

With the general advancement of consumerism the population as a whole will make it very difficult for any real estate practitioner who has the least inclination to scheme or connive his or her way to a closed transaction. In ever-increasing numbers, the public will see through all such approaches, even those that are not unethical albeit "unusual," and will reject them and their originators.

One might assume that the aforementioned aggregate wealth of tomorrow's consumers would ensure a continuation of today's level of compensation paid to real estate firms for competent services rendered.

Such may not be the case! Increasingly, during the last decade of the 20th century, consumers have become "bargain hunters." The pursuit of their parsimony will not extend to accepting flawed goods or sloppy service. Instead, they will evaluate closely the "valued added" or "value rendered" benefit of professional services and determine what level of payment is justified.

"BRAIN SURGERY IT AIN'T"

As one knowledgeable observer of the real estate industry explained, "Real estate brokerage is not brain surgery, but we expect to be paid like brain surgeons."

It is likely that the actual pricing structure of the future will be multifaceted, with a variety of brokerage compensation plans based on such criteria as price of the home, actual activities undertaken by the brokerage firm, length of time on the market, likelihood of additional business from the same client, condition of the overall market, etc.

The adaptability of tomorrow's consumers to a persistent environment of change should reward innovative real estate firms and agents. Clients and customers will no longer be wedded to traditional approaches in either marketing or seeking property. Instead, many will explore the advantages of working with practitioners who have a "different way of doing things" and will reward those who succeed with word-of-mouth praise that will generate considerably more business for the innovators. Of course, if the exploratory approach is less than promised, it will be quickly aborted, often in tandem with the firm or individual who proposed it.

To cope with the realities of tomorrow, in addition to relating to attitudinal, cultural and societal peculiarities, a real estate agent also will have to be conversant with and responsive to the macrocosmic alterations to American consumers that will alter the shape and substance of business activities in the forthcoming decades. Many of these are explained in detail in Chapter 5 of this book, which deals with demographics.

In addition, real estate agents wishing to succeed and prosper in the future should be knowledgeable about the marketplace ramifications of such factors as family size and structure, population mobility, job creation and location—specific lifestyle nuances attributable to central cities, suburbs, exurbs and rural areas.

FAMILY SIZE AND STRUCTURE

One need not be a statistical analyst nor a professional sociologist to understand that the basic social unit known as "the family" has undergone substantial changes in the last several decades and is quite likely to continue to do so in the foreseeable future.

Perhaps most noticeable is the fact that the number of individual persons in the family unit has been steadily declining—with dramatic effects on the real estate market. It's been a long time since most Americans had any notions that offspring were "cheaper by the dozen" or even more economical or desirable by the half-dozen. Today, at least among the vast majority of "traditional" husband and wife domestic units, two, or occasionally three, youngsters constitute a very "full" family.

At the same time, the "traditional" family mentioned above is being severely challenged as "the norm." Single-parent families—dominantly but not exclusively led by females— are the fastest growing segment of American social units. Domestic relationships not sanctioned by formal matrimony proliferate and steadily increase. Moreover, such live-in relationships are not necessarily of mixed gender.

Ignoring the ethical, social, moral or cultural outlook that individuals may have in support of or opposition to the alterations in family sizes and structures and concentrating solely on the effects these new families have on the real estate industry, one can easily recognize tremendous impacts.

For one, fewer family members generally means fewer rooms and less space in housing units, although it can dictate a *reallocation* of space to different lifestyles rather than a *diminution* (e.g., fewer bedrooms but larger "rec" rooms, entertainment centers or "grand rooms".

The structural adjustments should give notice to real estate practitioners that if they concentrate their efforts solely on servicing the "traditional" family, their base of potential clients and customers is likely to decline steadily. Instead, brokerage firms, and perhaps even individual agents need to focus on the new societal market "niches" created by alternative lifestyles. Some prominent real estate firms have already so adjusted and have offices or agent specialists who concentrate largely, if not solely, on housing for the gay and lesbian communities.

POPULATION MOBILITY

Americans have always been a population on the move. Settlers and adventurers followed the setting sun long before Horace Greeley advised young men to "go west." Corporate nomads dominated the ranks of upwardly mobile business types through much of the middle decades of the 20th century. But that situation too may be changing. To be sure, many U.S. citizens still dispatch themselves from a home in Miami to a residence in Seattle with the nonchalance that one might attribute to a move from 650 Elm Street to 810 Elm Street. But their numbers seem to be dwindling for a variety of reasons. Those whose relocations were largely a factor of corporate advancement are finding that their opportunities for transfer—and advancement—are, in the aggregate at least. fewer in number as the "downsizing" and "rightsizing" of the American business community takes its toll on middle- and upper-level-management positions.

Then too, attitudes have changed drastically. Not every employee leaps at the opportunity to climb the next rung or two on the corporate ladder if that ascent means relocating the family and/or converting from a comfortable to an unknown lifestyle.

According to results from Atlas Van Lines' 30th annual survey of corporate relocation policies, family bonds—more now than ever—are playing a major role in an employee's decision to relocate, and corporate America is responding with policies aimed at easing the transition. The survey notes that "family ties" is the number one reason employees reject a transfer. Nearly two-thirds, or 74.6 percent, of companies surveyed said that employees most often decline a relocation because they want to remain close to family members. That's up from the previous year's survey in which 54.7 percent of respondents listed "family ties" as the main reason for rejecting a relocation. This is a dramatic change in just three years. Then, cost-of-living was cited as the main reason for turning down a transfer. Cost-of-living is now the third most important consideration, behind a spouse's employment status.

Elder care assistance—another family issue—continues to be a relocation-related topic being addressed by today's businesses. Of the companies surveyed, 18 percent said they offer some type of elder care assistance. This includes everything from providing an employee with a list of nursing homes to moving the elderly relative to the employee's new location. A few companies are even reimbursing employees for outside care.

A new survey question reveals that international relocation success may rest on an employee's ability to adapt to new cultures. According to the survey, the main reason why international relocations fail is because of the employee's inability to adapt to his or her new surroundings. The main reason for declining an overseas relocation is lack of spousal or partner assistance.

Obviously, real estate firms whose profitability is directly related to an extensive amount of corporate relocation business had better reconfigure their business plans.

JOB CREATION

Tuccillo has frequently commented that "If you want to accurately predict the real estate activity in any area of the country, look at the job creation figures. If the community is generating jobs, the real estate market will enjoy prosperity. If the jobs are stagnant or declining, the real estate market is likely to head for the doldrums."

Technology is severely altering the landscape of American employment, along with the locations and environments of centers of employment. "Silicon valleys" and "high tech corridors" are "in," "rust belts" and "manufacturing meccas" are out.

Communication capabilities are rendering obsolete the need for physical proximity—even for workers assigned to the same project. The "assembly line" of the 21st Century will be connected by cybernetic interactions rather than by conveyor belts and instead of stretching the length of the shop floor may span several continents.

Increasingly, many workers will find that their commute from home to job has been reduced dramatically and now extends from bedroom to home office.

All of these factors and others currently unforeseen will severely alter the centers of population, business activity and real estate vibrancy in the decades ahead.

While the addition of a staff economist to the executive cadre of residential real estate firms is probably still a bit far-fetched, the notion of a realty company paying close and consistent attention to the movement of industry, commerce, employment levels and occupational pursuits is virtually a mandate for future success.

LOCATION

As discussed in Chapter 5, certain major conclusions can be drawn from anticipated future population trends as to which portions of the country will be growing faster or more slowly than others in the coming decades.

Amid all such valid macroanalysis, however, it is important to remember that "all real estate is local." The old bromide that the value of property is established by three things—location, location and location—can be applied to neighborhoods, cities, townships, counties, metropolitan centers and rural acreage just as validly as it is attributed to specific properties. As a result, one must be careful in applying broad generalities to the scope and direction of real estate activities within broad geographic sections of the nation, lest there be numerous pockets of "nonconforming" population centers within them.

Even in a broader sense, there is danger of substantial error in overgeneralizing. While it may be true to predict that suburban and exurban areas will grow and prosper as the center cities they surround stagnate or decline, examples can be found—Chicago, San Francisco, Miami, Manhattan, and numerous others, where the vibrancy of real estate activity in the core city has never been stronger.

The same localization applies to the preferences of individual consumers. While the broad generalities mentioned earlier in this chapter have statistical validity, they do not have infinite and universal application. As noted real estate expert Schlott puts it, "The marketplace in America is vast. There are 265 million people. We kind of lose sight of the fact that things are much different in Tulsa, Oklahoma than they are in Houston, Texas, than they are in San Diego. So, when we make statements about the industry, a lot of these changes are going to move in unusual ways in various locations."

CONSIDER NICHE MARKETING

Real estate people should not be admonished if they fail to respond to each of the myriad of potential industry and marketplace changes with detailed plans of action; however, they should be attentive to the fact that the overriding implication of such demographic data and sociological analysis is to pinpoint the necessity of developing and/or honing one or more specialized niches within the marketplace and addressing specific activities and promotional concentrations to the populations therein.

Mastering the field of niche marketing will be a process that differs among real estate firms, depending largely on the extensiveness and geographic scope of their operation.

Multioffice megabrokers will concentrate on many niches within their sphere of dominant influence. In effect, they will identify and specialize in a whole series of "minimarkets" within the broad spectrum of their entire company scope. Such divisions may be arranged so that whole offices concentrate on one or another niche or it may be that within each office, one or more agents or groups will hone in on specific categories of consumers.

In all of these considerations and concentrations, there is a need to examine closely what today's consumers contend will be their principal concerns for tomorrow and how they can be addressed by the professional real estate community in such a way as to increase the dependency of the home-buying and home-selling public on the industry practitioner.

One must remember that because, indeed, the consumer is in "the driver's seat," if the vehicle fails to perform, there are other options. Drivers can acquire other vehicles, or other real estate agents, with dispatch and ease. Or just as they can revert to other forms of transportation—cabs, public transit, even walking—so too may they initiate their real estate business with a lender or a home builder or either buy from or become a FSBO.

Successful real estate firms of the future will be "driven" by consumers to new levels of superior performance and service.

CHAPTER 7

Agent: A Profession in Question

"I don't think consumers will continue to accept the level of service they get today."

Gary Daniels, president, Harmon Publishing Co.

"I think that the consumer is going to preselect, they are going to do some of their screening, they are going to do some tire kicking long before they see the real estate professional."

John Moore, president, Genesis Relocation Services

"We need to be proactive because if we are just reacting to the outside, an external force is going to come in and we won't be able to run fast enough to catch up with it."

Linda Hondros, president, Hondros College.

The consumer will be the driving force of the real estate industry from here on out, or at least, into the foreseeable future. Once upon a time, the real estate professional controlled access to real estate information. With that control came the ability to call the shots. The consumer had little power in the real estate transaction. They could

- attempt to sell their homes themselves (be a FSBO),
- buy from someone who was selling a home by himself or herself (buy from a FSBO),
- be one of those people who have a real estate license just to buy and sell their own properties,
- or they could entrust the transaction to a real estate professional.

Most statistics demonstrate that about 80 percent of homes bought or sold involved an independent real estate professional in the transaction. "This percentage has remained remarkably steady over the years," says National Association of REALTORS® spokeswoman Elizabeth Johnson.

Those days when the real estate professional controlled access to real estate information are gone forever. Consumers can get information directly from the Internet. Mortgage banking companies are getting involved in transactions. Even credit card companies and airlines now have programs that involve them in the real estate transaction. Who or what will be next? Hondros's statement about the need to be proactive is quickly becoming passe. Can we catch up with the outside force that has started to invade the industry? The answer is yes, but we can't afford to wait much longer if we are to do it!

WHAT DO CONSUMERS WANT FROM THE AGENT?

The top 7 of 12 consumer and demographic trends for 1995 identified in the Abelson Trends Report are consumer-related trends (see Table 7.1). Six of the top 7 trends identified in the same report for the year 2000 are also consumer trends.

The consumer demands better, more knowledgeable/professional agents was the number one consumer/demographic trend in 1995. Consumers want agents to have the answers to all their home-buying needs. What specifics do you have on the schools that service this neighborhood? Are there any preexisting conditions on this house? Is this really priced right or is there a lot of room for negotiations to lower the price of the home? Is this home the best value on the market today for the needs that I expressed to you? What effect will future development have on this property/ this neighborhood? These are just some of the issues consumers expect from today's agent.

TABLE 7.1 Abelson TrendWatch Index™

Consumer/Demographic Trends	1995 Index†	Rank	2000 Index	Rank
Consumer demands better, more knowledgeable/ professional agents	130	1	77	3
Public gains access to MLS	75	2*	118	1
Consumer increases demands on agents	75	2*	53	4
Consumer more astutely negotiates REALTOR® fees	71	4	49	5
Consumer direct access of home purchase information increases	53	5	106	2
Consumer needs exceeding skills of agent	41	6	19	9
Consumer increases demands on brokerage firm	33	7	28	7
Needs regarding residential housing shift as demographics change	32	8	26	8
Residential housing needs shift as elderly population grows	22	9	45	6
Changes in American culture impact agent recruiting	16	10	14	11
Closer relationships occur between brokerage firms and consumer	13	11	18	10
Residential housing needs shift as cultural diversity increases	3	12	9	12

©1996, Michael Abelson.

*Tied.

†The Index is a score developed by Dr. Abelson from his national research of real estate industry trends. It is used to determine the level of importance of each trend as ranked by the industry experts who participated in his research.

There was a tie for second place. The first number two consumer/demographic trend in the year 1995 was that the public gains access to the MLS. We are already seeing the impact this trend is having. That impact will continue to increase as the consumer gains more access and shares control of real estate information. The consumer increases demands on the agent (the second #2 trend), the consumer more astutely negotiates real estate fees (trend #4) and the consumer direct access of home purchase information increases (trend #5) round out the top five 1995 trends identified by the Abelson Trends Report™.

Even more telling is what the report says will occur by the year 2000. The consumer will have access to the MLS data (trend #1 in the year 2000) and the consumer will increasingly gain direct access to home purchase information (trend #2 in the year 2000). We are now seeing both of these trends. In addition, the consumer will more astutely negotiate real estate fees (trend #5 in the year 2000), the consumer will increase demands on agents (trend #4 in the year 2000) (via quality service, types of services offered, etc.) and the consumer will demand better, more knowledgeable/professional agents (trend #3 by the year 2000) round out the top five year 2000 trends.

We are seeing increasingly educated consumers who are willing to use their knowledge and newly learned technologies to personally get involved in the real estate transaction. How the real estate professional helps them throughout the transaction is the crucial test of quality service to the consumer. Real estate professionals in the future will have to give advice on how consumers can get the most out of the Internet to help prepare them for the home-selling or home-buying process. Real estate professionals will also fully explain the home-buying or home-selling process and demonstrate what they do that adds value to the process. A list of all the steps in the buying or selling process, the role of the agent and when it is appropriate for the agent and consumer to interact and discuss issues are both excellent ways to start contributing true value-added quality service to the real estate professional and consumer relationship.

Consumer behavior and expectations are contributing to soul searching within the industry. Schlott paints this picture about the current situation: "We looked at a dark cloud, and we're out on the water. We are a rudderless group right now." This rudderlessness comes from many issues facing the industry; consumers' needs and their reaction to real estate industry actions are definite core issues.

Agents currently take several approaches when working with the consumer. First, they provide information to the consumer. In most situations, the real estate professional still has more information than does the consumer. Second, they take the consumer's order. They list the house or they help the consumer find a house and then negotiate/write the contract. Third, they talk about the high quality of service they give the consumer. These are the behaviors the consumer is most likely to see when interacting with a real estate professional. Is this worth 5 to 7 percent of the cost of the home? Many consumers now question this. In fact, a May 10, 1996, *Wall Street Journal* article reported that a study of consumers found that 52 percent preferred not to use an agent because they did not want to pay the agent's commission.

If this strategy continues, agents might as well pack up and sell the farm. The consumer will have access to more and more information. The role of the agent in the consumer's mind is decreasing in importance. Anyone can take the order. There is no need to pay 5 to 7 percent commission for that. Finally, just talking about quality service won't make the consumer happy. There is a need to deliver real, quantifiable quality service.

WHAT CAN THE REAL ESTATE AGENT DO TO
SURPASS CONSUMER EXPECTATIONS AND SATISFY?

Consumers of the future will have the information and, unless things change, will personally discount the amount of effort and level of service they see the agent offer. The agent in the future will be delivering quality service. They will do this by adding value to the information already available to the consumer and by adding value to the home-buying and home-selling transaction. The agent will add value in at least five ways.

First, the real estate professional will be sorting through information that is available and giving the consumer quality information that more closely meets the needs of that particular consumer. There is so much information available now to the consumer that the consumer is starting to get overwhelmed. Information will be increasingly available in the future. The astute real estate professional will assist the consumer by "qualifying the consumer's needs" and then helping them find or giving them the information that meets those needs. Real estate professionals used to have to qualify the buyer's/seller's needs in buying or selling the home. When they were assisting the buyer, they also had to assess the consumer's purchasing power. The real estate professional's job is still the same, but now it also includes giving consumers the information that meets their needs and helping them find the information that is most pertinent to their needs. The agent of today and tomorrow will be a buffer around all this information and save the consumer time, effort and the frustration associated with sorting through all this information.

Second, the real estate professional will be interpreting and integrating the information. In other words, the real estate professional will turn information into usable knowledge. Consumers can get the information on their own. Unless the consumers have been through the home-buying process numerous times, they still need help understanding what all that information means. The real estate professional should not allow the consumer or the availability of all this information to intimidate them. Take the opportunity to show consumers how you can use this information in ways beyond their thoughts. You will have added value to the relationship by demonstrating your expertise. Consumers who value information especially value someone who can effectively and efficiently *use* that information. These consumers will more highly value the knowledgeable real estate professional.

Third, the real estate professional will be adding to this knowledge by showing "wisdom" about the marketplace, the property, the real estate transaction, etc. Wisdom occurs when someone shows significant insight beyond the information. Effectively identify the buyers'/sellers' needs above and beyond consumers' awareness of their needs, and then use that information in their home-buying and home-selling experience. For example, note that the buyer really wants a low maintenance property, even though his or her past property was far from maintenance free. Show the consumer the pros and cons of certain information either you or he or she have available that relates to that newly realized need. This is "wisdom." This is a value-added service.

Fourth, the real estate professional will give true quality service. This means speedily meeting the needs of the consumer; and keeping in contact with the consumer throughout the entire transaction and after the transaction. Also, the real estate professional will do things that keep the home buyer and eventual seller emotionally attached to that particular real estate professional. As people move less often and believe they need a real estate professional to help them in this move-less-often, it will become increasingly important to capture those who do move or people they know in their influence circles who will be moving. Follow-up mechanisms will need to be put in place to effectively meet these needs.

Fifth, the real estate professional in the future will need to offer the consumer all the services the consumer is interested in. A "shopping" list of quality services offered by the brokerage or the agent can be given to the home buyer or seller. Let consumers choose their interests. "Give them more of a menu approach to services rather than a discounted approach to services," stresses industry consultant Jenny. Because most agents do not like to deal with these ancillary services, it makes sense that brokers offer to service the real estate agent's client/customer on this dimension. Car dealerships have several people who "sell" the financing, the maintenance insurance and other value-added services. Real estate offices are already offering this type of service with mortgages and other services. This is an area of growth for both the agent and the broker and should be pursued.

The real estate agent of the future will have greater services expected of them by the more knowledgeable and demanding consumer. To effectively compete in the marketplace, people should consider being more flexible, being more willing to actually change, being better listeners and being quicker learners.

HOW ARE COMPANIES DEALING WITH CONSUMER NEEDS?

Remaining in the real estate industry—both in the recent past and in the future—requires the desire to invest in the business and to make appropriate decisions regarding that investment. As we have seen, significant changes and demands brought about by consumer needs and technological advancements have led to a need to invest in the business all the time. This need to invest to remain profitable will increase. The competitive market pressures have

FIGURE 7.1 Franchise Affiliations

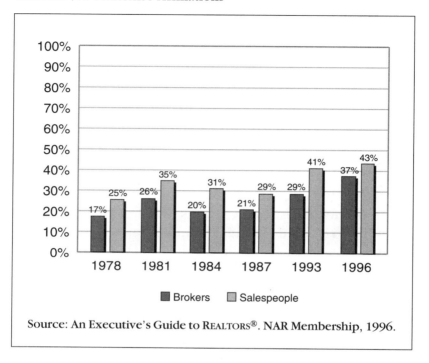

Source: An Executive's Guide to REALTORS®. NAR Membership, 1996.

resulted in various alternative approaches for brokerage companies to meet consumer needs.

These alternative approaches have several underlying characteristics. They allow for (1) more cost effectiveness through the use of technology, (2) marketing/brand-name awareness and/or (3) the development/acquisition of quality assets (people, facilities, equipment). The following are seven approaches that use these three underlying characteristics.

Franchise Approach

One approach is to affiliate with an organization that brings these three things to the marketplace. One way to do that is through a quality franchise. Franchise affiliation has increased rather steadily since 1978 (see Figure 7.1). In

TABLE 7.2   Brokers Perception of Effect of Franchise Affilliation on Sales and Profits: (Percentage Distribution of Affiliated Firms

		Improved %	No Appreciable Effect %	Diminished %	Too Soon To Tell %
	1996	84	16	*	NA
	1992	90	10	*	NA
Sales	1990	79	15	1	6
	1986	83	11	1	5
	1996	79	18	3	NA
Profits	1992	79	17	4	NA
	1990	70	18	5	7
	1986	67	20	6	8

*Less than one percent

NA: Not Applicable

Source: National Association of REALTORS® Profile of Real Estate Firms, 1996.

1978, 17 percent of the brokers and 25 percent of the agents were affiliated with a franchise. Nine years later, in 1987, 21 percent of firms and 29 percent of the salespeople were affiliated with a franchise. Nine years after that, in 1996, 37 percent of the brokers and 43 percent of the salespeople were affiliated with a franchise. Franchises bring cost effectiveness through allowing member companies to use their technology services (e.g., web pages and on-line property listings), brand-name awareness through use of the franchise name and reputation, and the development and acquisition of quality assets through training classes, recruiting programs and suggested approaches to increasing market presence that are made available through the franchisor.

Joining a franchise has resulted in broker perception of both increased sales and profitability (see Table 7.2). From 1986 until the most recent statistics compiled by the NAR in 1996, a minimum of 79 percent of franchisees say their

TABLE 7.3 Broker Perception of Effect of Franchise Affiliation on Firm Operations (Percentage Distribution of Affiliated Firms)

	Improved Considerably %	Improved Moderately %	No Effect %	Diminished %
Advertising Exposure	51	39	10	*
Obtaining Listings	52	40	8	*
Making Sales	43	41	16	*
Recruiting Sales Associates	41	41	17	1
Developing Management Skills	42	38	20	*
Name Recognition	73	21	5	1
Profitability	33	46	18	3
Training	45	37	17	1
Acquiring New Technology	45	32	23	*

*Less than one percent

Source: National Association of REALTORS® Profile of Real Estate Firms, 1996.

sales increased and at least 67 percent said profits increased through the franchise relationship. These are very interesting statistics.

At least 50 percent of these same firms report that operations issues such as name recognition, advertising exposure, and obtaining listings improved considerably (see Table 7.3). At worst, only 23 percent of firms stated that one of the nine different operations issues examined in the NAR Profile of Real Estate Firms was not at least moderately improved by getting involved with a franchise. Please keep in mind that these data are collected after people affiliate with the franchise and their response may be the result of their rationalizing and justifying their decisions to join a franchise. Although some of the results may be attributed to this rationalization, the numbers suggest that joining a franchise has positive outcomes.

Large Company Network Approach

A second approach to obtaining (1) cost effectiveness through the use of technology, (2) marketing/brand-name awareness and/or (3) the development/acquisition of quality assets (people, facilities, equipment) is to join a network of existing companies. The Vision and Realty Alliance (merger of both the Mastermind, and the Dozen) are examples of companies that have joined together to have the above-mentioned and other needs met.

These types of associations have the benefit of not having to pay a franchise fee. In addition, these networks are usually fairly selective on the companies who are allowed to join their ranks. This allows for maintaining a certain quality standard. Members of these networks share certain types of information, inform each other of certain types of programs/services that they have found the most effective and have such common programs as top-performer retreats. In addition, some of these networks evaluate fellow network members on a regular basis. This allows for outside experts to examine company systems and approaches and give suggestions on how to better manage the company.

There are no current statistics to suggest that joining a large network such as those listed above increases sales or profits, but one suspects that affiliation with these meganetworks is beneficial. The fact that the Mastermind and the Dozen have merged to form an even larger and potentially stronger organization, the Realty Alliance, speaks to the perceived benefit of joining such a network.

Technology Approach

A third approach to dealing with consumer needs and the increasing competition in the marketplace is to increase greater internal efficiency—whether a member of a franchise, large network or neither. Increasingly, technology is used in the office to meet consumer and agent needs (Table 7.4 lists ways to use computer technology). Fifteen

TABLE 7.4   Computer Software Currently Used by Real Estate Firms

Primary Uses	Percent of Frequency/Ranking of Software Use		
	All Firms Percent/ Ranking	Firms with 5 or Fewer Agents Percent/ Ranking	Firms with 50 or More Agents Percent/ Ranking
Word Processing	89/1	88/1	95/1T
Multiple-Listing Software'	77/2	69/2	95/1T
Accounting/Payroll/ Financial	61/3	56/3	90/4
Comparative Market Analysis	54/4	40/5	92/3
Spreadsheets	51/5	49/4	67/8
Desktop Publishing	43/6T	36/7T	75/6T
Communications	43/6T	36/7T	75/6T
Graphics/Presentation Software	40/8	30/8	77/5
Loan Analysis	36/9	28/9	52/10
Property Management	26/10	25/10	30/9
Other Uses			
Contact Management	22	15	57/9
Other	23	25	20
Information Systems	15	11	37
Time Management	14	11	22
Mapping Software/ Geographic	—	—	---

T = Tied

Source: Modified from Table 37, page 45, National Assocation of REALTORS®, Profile of Real Estate Firms, 1996.

different types of uses are identified. Table 7.4 shows data on the use of these 15 types of software programs for all real estate firms, for firms with 5 or fewer agents and for firms with 50 or more agents. (For more information about technology use by firms between these two extremes, see Table 37 in the Profile of Real Estate Firms, 1996, by the National Association of REALTORS®.)

We can see some interesting applications for software through examining Table 7.4. The first two choices are the same for small firms and large firms. They both use word processing and multiple-listing services software on their computers. Many of the other uses have similar rankings. The biggest difference seems to be that the larger firms use their computers much more for graphic presentations and for contact management than do the smaller firms. These may be areas in which the small firms should consider focusing more of their resources.

Integrative Computer Software Approach

Another trend in the application of computer technology is to have bundles that integrate across computing functions. Moore Data has purchased several companies where their software is supposed to "talk" well with each other. They and other companies are having some difficulties meeting the needs of the real estate office in actually delivering on expectations. A new concept of having software systems networked with each other, even though the softwares are not owned by the same company, has been instituted. Connections Plus has developed a system that allows for multiple software applications to effectively communicate with each other. For example, front office, back office and MLS data can be effectively accessed from the same network of software. This system and concept only allows softwares with proven records and high quality/reputations to tie into the network. This approach gives real estate firms the option of choosing the applications they want to implement in their companies without the expense of buying all the software applications at the same time or ever. This new concept has a great deal of promise in its flexibility, cost and ability to meet the needs of the real estate professional. Time will tell how effectively it is implemented.

Standardized Services Approach

A fifth trend that has recently begun is for brokers to offer more services to their sales agents that better standardize and more efficiently use certain aspects of the residential sales transaction. One example of this new approach is having the broker telemarket to get leads for sales agents. In the past, agents were solely responsible to follow up on leads that either they or the organization generated. The extent to which these referrals were converted to actual sales was typically low. New agents would staff the telephones ("floor call" or "floor duty") in hopes of generating a lead. A study by Abelson & Company in 1991 showed the average top producer (someone earning more than $90,000 in personal earnings annually) took floor duty an average of two hours a week. The low producers (those earning $15,000 to $30,000 a year in personal income) took floor duty an average of seven hours a week. Thus, the person who was most likely to convert this new customer into a sale was out selling other people, not sitting at the call desk. The low-producing agent was the one handling those leads calling into the office. This approach has a history of very low conversion rates. These new leads management programs are showing conversion rates many times higher. Brokers are offering more services like these as a way to gain more efficiency in the office and to more profitably serve the consumer, who is increasingly demanding more from the real estate professional.

Merger Approach

A sixth trend firms are using to deal with consumer and other demands is to get out of the business. Laurie Moore-Moore, co-editor of *RealTRENDS,* states that the number of residential real estate brokerages have decreased from approximately 150,000 in 1990 to approximately 90,000 now. That is a huge decrease in a relatively short period of time. Industry merger experts, like David Cocks, co-founder of CompensationMaster, assist dozens of mergers each year. This merger trend of downsizing will continue for the conceivable future. As the brokers increase in age along with the rest of the general population (see Chapter 5), more owners will attempt to sell their assets (their businesses) instead of being consumed with fighting the changing industry. Other firms will see this as an opportunity to increase their own economies of scale through merging assets (salespeople, market image, etc.) within the same marketplace. Expect in the year 2000 to see even fewer brokerage companies as those who have the strategies, systems and determination continue to enhance their position while the others look for acceptable alternatives to maximize their current situations.

Single License Approach

The seventh and final approach is the trend to offer a single real estate license, namely a broker license. The State of Colorado has already implemented this approach. Several other states are now studying whether to follow Colorado.

Abelson & Company and the Institute for Community Research at the University of Tampa completed a joint study in December 1996 funded by the Florida Real Estate Commission to examine the competencies of both real estate brokers and agents. This very extensive study included both focus groups and a survey mailed to 2,000 agents and 2,000 brokers throughout the State of Florida. Some pertinent highlights of this 51-page report are shown in Table 7.5.

The study examined 85 competency areas identified in the focus groups for agents and 176 competency areas identified in the focus groups for brokers. A portion of the study ranks the level of importance and the difficulty level of mastering each of the 85 and 176 competencies. Table 7.5 presents the first 15 areas for both agents and brokers in the order of their importance. It is interesting to note that 10 of the top 15 competencies for both agents and brokers are very similar. The table also notes which agent and broker areas appear in the other's top 15 competency areas list.

Negotiation skills, communication skills, agency issues, the sales contract, the selling process and disclosures are all ranked in the top 15 by both agents and brokers. Areas where only the agent listed the competency in the top 15 include the agent focusing on working with customers/ clients/brokers, assessing buyer needs, marketing self/service/property and understanding and completing forms. Areas where only the broker listed the competency in the top 15 include ethical conduct in real estate, escrow management, effective written communication, knowledge of business management and agency disclosure form and timing. Many of these areas were listed further down in the other's list.

As mentioned, many of the most important areas of the agent and the broker are similar. Those agent roles not included in the broker areas deal with people interrelationships, not anything typically related to required real estate licensing laws. Apparently, if brokers were asked what is important in their role as salespersons we would hear them discuss the need to be competent while working with customer and clients as well as assessing buyer needs (areas not reported in the top 15 broker areas in the study). These areas do appear further down in the list of 176 competencies.

The bottom line? Agent and broker competencies related to the consumer look fairly similar, at least among the top areas identified in the study. It may make sense from a com-

TABLE 7.5 Broker/Agency Competency Study*

	Agent Competencies			Broker Competencies	
Order of Importance	Item	Comparable Broker Item	Order of Importance	Item	Comparable Broker Item
1	Working with customers and clients		1	Ethical conduct in real estate	
2	Negotiation skills	9	2	The real estate contract	8
3	Process from sale to close	6	3	Effective verbal communication	5 and 13
4	Offers and counteroffers	9	4	Escrow account management	
5	Listening skills	3	5	Effective written communication	
6	Disclosures	8	6	Process from contract to closing	3
7	Closing costs, fees and taxes	7 and 14	7	Closing transaction	
8	Obligations of parties to contract	2	8	Disclosing defects	7
9	Assessing buyer needs		9	Negotiation skills and knowledge	6 and 14
10	Concept of agency	10 and 13	10	Agency license law	4
11	Marketing self, service and property		11	Required documents for closing	10
12	Understanding and completing forms		12	Knowledge of business management	7
13	Sales and communication skills	3 and 5	13	Concept of agency	
14	Required disclosures		14	Basic closing statements and costs	10
15	Working with agents and brokers		15	Agency disclosure form and timing	7

*Performed by Abelson & Company and the Institute for Community Research at the University of Tampa, 1996. Funded by the Florida Real Estate Commission.

petency standpoint to have a unified license. If this did occur, it may also improve the professionalism of the real estate professional. Real estate people pride themselves in the designations they receive, even though most consumers have no concept of what the designations mean. Both of the above enhancements (expanded competencies and a unified license) may contribute to an improved impression of the real estate professional by the demanding consumer.

WHAT THE FUTURE HOLDS FOR BEST SERVING CONSUMERS

The consumer in the future will be increasingly demanding, more knowledgeable about the real estate transaction and have direct access to more information. They will not see the value added of the real estate professional and will negotiate to decrease the commission rate because of this. Consumers will be "king" and will be the driving force, so their needs must be met by the real estate professional or consumers *will go somewhere else* to have their needs met. Technology will be an increasingly plausible alternative. New technologies that are about to be introduced into the market and that are currently on the drawing board will be real threats to the real estate process as it is managed now.

In order to survive, thrive and satisfy the consumer's needs, the successful brokerage company and agent will be doing business differently.

- High tech and high touch will go hand-in-hand. The role of the agent is to use technology to offer a warm, personal touch to the home buyer or seller. Technology cannot do it alone yet (by the year 2005 and no later than 2010 technology may be able to do it by itself).
- Agents need to educate people on the services they do offer so the consumer understands and "buys into" the agent's and broker's role in the transaction. That role is

of information buffer, knowledge giver and wisdom sharer. Agents will need to educate the consumer on this value-added role by making them aware of all the services the agent and broker can give even if the consumer chooses not to use particular services. Something as simple as giving and explaining to the consumer a list of all the agent and broker services available is a start to this education process. Real estate professionals are a very industrious group and will develop other ways to get "buy in" from the consumer.

- Agents and brokers will need to give true quality service to the consumer: timely and speedy service. Terrific follow-up to recapture consumers when they next enter the home purchase process will help tremendously.

- Brokerages will use various approaches in order to create (1) cost effectiveness, (2) marketing/brand-name awareness and/or (3) the development/acquisition of quality assets (people, facilities, equipment). They will use franchising, company network systems, technology, integrative computer software, standardized services and/or mergers and acquisitions.

Will someone or something replace the agent?

The agent is already being replaced by technology and the natural competitive market forces. The way for the agent to survive and thrive is to change with the consumer's needs by taking the following steps:

- Regain control of the transaction by letting consumers believe they are in control of the information. Of course, smart agents will share only pertinent information with the consumer as they share knowledge and wisdom. This is the way to regain control of the process, by giving value-added services that are perceived by the consumer.

- Do those parts of the transaction that only agents can do and let the efficiencies of technology or human assistants do the rest. Let the broker telemarket through the use of in-office computer software for a small fee. It is much cheaper than having the agent doing it. Let the part- or full-time assistant do those things the agent either dislikes doing, is not good at doing or are too time-consuming. The transaction of the future will be much more efficient. Those who fight this will be out of business eventually. Learn how to use the opportunities available to create efficiencies and be ahead of the curve.
- Let the broker get back into the business by offering services that are viable for both the agent and the consumer. This will lead to even greater cost effectiveness and allow everyone to be profitable.
- Do those things that enhance the consumer's impression of professionalism in the real estate industry. Single license laws may be an answer for this. Search out other ways to have the consumer value the real estate agent and broker as true professionals.

"We are getting a considerably higher educated personnel, much more sincere, much more professional, much more customer oriented," states Maria Bunting, co-president of Windermere Real Estate. It couldn't have happened at a better time.

CHAPTER 8

Are Brokers and Agents Overpaid?

Straight Split Plans Based on Points, Sides or GCI
Retroactive Plans
Incremental Plans
100 Percent Plans
High Split Plans with Charge Backs
Rolling Average Plans
Combined Schedules
Salary
and much, much more!

So which plan do you want today? If it does not suit you, which plan do you want tomorrow?

No wonder the latest data show that tens of thousands of residential brokerage firms are not profitable.

A 1995 National Association of REALTORS® study reported that approximately 25 percent of all firms were not profitable and that occurred during a relatively good year in real estate. What happens in the lean years?

Another study by the Rocky Mountain Consulting Group, of 1,200 people attending their seminars, found more than 50 percent said their brokerages did not make a profit. Of these, 77 percent of the owners and managers feel their companies need to modify their policies of sharing expenses with their salespeople.

Add to this, consumer sentiment that agents make too much money, and we have a problem.

The real estate industry by nature and design is a very entrepreneurial group. The diversity of compensation plans demonstrates this. Brokers are entrepreneurial and so are agents. In a desire to meet the needs of the entrepreneurial agent, the broker in many cases has "given away the shop." Brokerages are experiencing great levels of frustration and confusion concerning their inability to maintain a profit, yet they have been willing to pay agents an ever-increasing piece of the resource pie to attract and keep them.

There once was a dry cleaner who never figured out how much it actually cost him to clean a garment. He just knew that if he dry-cleaned enough garments he would be profitable. So in order to get the consumer's business, he made less profit per garment; he lowered his dry-cleaning price. It worked. The number of garments he was cleaning increased dramatically. He was very happy with this additional market share. The day he closed his business for good, because he was losing money, was the day he admitted to himself that his price to clean each garment was more than the price he was charging his clientele.

How many real estate firms are following this same principle? Increase market share at all costs. If you have to have a couple "loss leaders" (high producing agents who make more and/or use more resources than they bring in) that's OK. Their association with the company will bring in more business and make the company more money. The problem is, all the other agents want the same treatment of receiving higher commissions—and many receive the higher commissions. After a while the broker begins to realize that he can't afford to stay in business. He is losing money on many agents and can't make up the difference from the other agents.

The outcome is the mass exodus of brokers from the industry. Those companies that have discovered how to be profitable are purchasing those that have not. The merger-and-acquisition trend has been escalating each year and will continue.

WHY ARE REAL ESTATE FIRMS NOT PROFITABLE?

There are numerous reasons why real estate firms are not profitable. The primary reasons are closely related to certain assumptions and attitudes of company managements. A primary reason is that owners are very entrepreneurial. Entrepreneurs are typically a very optimistic lot. They believe that they can deal with long-term issues later and typically will take risks when dealing with short-term opportunities. So when there is a chance of getting a top agent, there is a tremendous temptation to do so, whatever the cost. When you have bright agents that see how the system works, it does not take very long before their entrepreneurial spirit lets them take advantage of the opportunities.

Over the last 10 or 15 years, brokers have allowed themselves to "buy into" this system. As Mike Brodie, past president of the Texas Association of REALTORS® and currently at Keller Williams in Dallas, says, "I think real estate is getting to be like sports; it's almost a free agency market for top agents. We've got to get away from this." The future regarding this may be brighter than the recent past. According to Steve Neuman, director of consulting for Compensation-Master, the industry leader in compensation systems, "Brokers are realizing that they have hurt themselves and their competitors by offering more and more competitive plans. They are now realizing there is a need for them to take back control of their own business destiny."

A second management attitude that has contributed to less profitability is that brokers have focused on the agent as their only client. Commission plans have focused solely on meeting the needs of the agent and have not looked at how plans can be developed that (1) meet the broker's needs and, more importantly, (2) meet the consumer's needs. Because of this, agent reward systems promote quick consumer service to generate as many closed sides as possible. One way to get more closed sides is to have new and inexperienced independent contractors buy and sell with a few friends and relatives and hope we never run out of new agents. A second way is to support agents who close mega-sides regardless of the type of true quality service they give to their clientele. After all, for both these cases, the bottom line is the bottom line.

The outcome is that consumers frequently do not get the service and treatment they are increasingly receiving from other service industries. Daniels puts it this way. "The whole process is up in the air. No matter what else is going on it's going to come down to the service delivery to the consumer, and today, that quality is all over the map."

A third management philosophy is the attitude of the replaceability of the agent. Agents are not valued as true assets, just walking market share. When agents are not valued, they can be treated like they are staff on an assembly line—Henry Ford's approach. If they don't work out, let's just get another one and hope the new one works out. After all, they don't cost us anything. They are easily replaced.

That statement could not be further from the truth. The wrong person in the office can cost the broker $10,000s in lost opportunities, aggravated clientele and underutilized midlevel salespeople who could easily and more effectively handle more business. This philosophy also leads to brokers not selecting appropriate people to work in real estate. Anyone will do. If they pass the mirror test (if a mirror is put under their nose and the mirror fogs up), they become an agent. This is especially frustrating because there are systems available in the marketplace to assist brokers identify people who have profiles that strongly suggest they *will* succeed or *will not* succeed in selling real estate.

The "walking market share" replaceability attitude leads to just the opposite action. We can't let someone who has that much market share leave no matter what the expense. Brokers then "give away the farm" and get in bidding wars with other brokers. When they lose the bidding war, they then go after one of the agents at the office that won the war. The broker's goal is to "capture" the market share lost to the competitor. Wow. What a concept. Agents must love brokers fighting over their perceived inability to replace their agent's market share. You can't blame agents for taking advantage of the situation. Why do brokers get into this self-defeating cycle?

A fourth philosophy is the attitude of the broker's role in the office. Are they selling managers or managers who manage? Many smaller offices, and some big offices, use the rationale that the manager needs to sell to be profitable. If that is the case, why be a manager at all? Why not just be an agent?

When managers sell, they are in competition with their agents in two ways. First, time they could spend helping their agents produce is spent in personal sales. Second, they can be competing for common clientele in the marketplace with their agents, and that is duplication of effort. The reason people invest money is to leverage their time while the money works for them. The reason to invest your money in a business is so you can use your money to leverage your time so your money works for you through the business. The bottom line? Leverage your time through managing others so several of your staff can be working for you at the same time. Give them some value added in the relationship by being an effective manager so the better agents want to stay. When three, four, five, ten people work for you and have the necessary skills and the loyalty to you to stay and produce, in most situations you will make much more than if you also sell.

The key to all four philosophies is to develop the right reward system so the brokerage can afford to spend the resources necessary to attract, select, train, compensate, maintain and manage the best people possible in order for everyone to maximize or at least satisfy their needs for "wealth."

CURRENT REWARD SYSTEMS

Management literature tells us there are several key components to reward systems that work.

Reward systems need to be

- easily understood;
- fair (appropriate level of reward for appropriate level of work);
- equitable (people doing the same behavior get the same reward);
- designed to reward the desired behavior;
- received soon enough after the correct behavior so the person receiving the reward knows which behavior they are receiving the reward for;
- developed so the reward is desired by the person receiving the reward (people prefer different things as rewards; some prefer material things like money; others prefer intrinsic things like opportunities to excel, recognition, the pride of being first/respected/good/ etc.);
- flexible so the rewards can more easily meet multiple needs of the same person/multiple needs of multiple people; and
- many forms of rewards, not just money.

The more of the above criteria that is met by the reward system, the better that reward system will work.

The real estate industry has a wealth of current reward systems. Most focus on a specific compensation (mostly money) and use a compensation plan with some flexibility. Data on the frequency of usage of some of these plans, from a 1996 National Association of REALTORS® report, appear in Table 8.1. Examples of specific plans follow:

- *Straight commission plans,* which are based on the number of points you obtain (different types of sales have different point values), the number of sides you

TABLE 8.1 Compensation Structure of REALTORS®
(Percentage Distribution)

	All* REALTORS® %	Brokers/ Broker Associates %	Sales Agents %
Percentage Commission Split	74	65	80
100% Commission	17	22	15
Straight Salary	2	2	2
Salary Plus Share of Profits	2	3	1
Commission Plus Share of Profits	3	6	2
Share of Profits Only	1	1	1
Mean Starting Percentage Commission Split	57	60	56
Median Starting Percentage Commission Split	55	60	50
Mean Year End Commission Split	63	68	61
Median Year End Commission Split	63	70	60

*Because of rounding error, columns may not add to 100%.

Source: National Association of REALTORS® Profile of Real Estate Firms, 1996.

have sold or the agent's Gross Commission Income (GCI)

- *Retroactive commission plans,* where agents get money back on lower levels of sales as they reach each higher level
- *Incremental plans,* where every time agents sell at a different threshold level they receive a higher commission

- *100 percent plans,* where agents have certain costs/ fees they pay the broker regardless of how much they sell
- *High split plans with charge backs,* where agents have a high split to start, but certain expenses are charged back to the agents for them to pay
- *Rolling average plans,* where agents start at their previous commission level, which is higher than zero GCI, and this higher level is used to calculate the commission
- *Combined schedules,* which occur when a different commission rate is used and scheduled for different types of sales activities
- *Base plus plans,* which start at a certain commission percent and at different levels the agent gets a certain percent more commission
- Commission plus share of profits
- Salary
- Salary plus share of profits
- Share of profits only

Most of the currently used plans are some form of the percentage commission split plan (used by 74 percent of the companies responding to the NAR study) or a 100 percent commission plan (used by 17 percent of the companies responding to the same study).

FRINGE BENEFIT PLANS

An area of compensation within the industry that has been receiving additional consideration recently is fringe benefits. Independent contractors, which account for almost all of the salespeople in the industry, traditionally do not receive fringe benefits by companies. As a way to create loyalty and instill commitment to the organization, more and more firms are offering salespeople fringe benefits similar to the types of benefits they have offered administrative staff for some time.

The most frequently offered fringe benefit seems to be errors and omission insurance. The extent to which this is offered varies depending on the size of the real estate firm. Firms that have more than 50 agents offer this as a benefit 95 percent of the time. Firms with 5 or fewer agents offer this benefit only 45 percent of the time. All firms surveyed and reported in the 1996 NAR Profile of Real Estate Firms offered this benefit 62 percent of the time.

Health insurance was and is another benefit offered on a rather regular basis. Firms with 51 or more agents offer this benefit to their independent contractors and employed licensees 48 percent of the time. Their administrative staff have this as a benefit 67 percent of the time. Firms with 5 or fewer agents offer this benefit 15 percent of the time or less to each of the three types of staff. All firms offer this benefit to administrative staff (21 percent), independent contractors (19 percent) and employed licensees (15 percent), a little more than do those who own the smallest firms.

Group term life insurance, profit sharing and pension plans are other fringe benefits offered, but these are offered on a relatively infrequent basis. Moore sees several of these benefits being offered more often in the future. He believes that "profit sharing, preferred stock, and any kind of options of this nature make sense. Whenever you tie long-term profit of the company to the company's benefits, you buy the loyalty of the staff to the company. They have to stay there in order to get the benefit." See Table 8.2 for more information on these and the previously mentioned fringe benefits available in the real estate industry.

TABLE 8.2 Fringe Benefits Offered by Real Estate Firms

	All Firms %	5 or less %	6–10 %	11–20 %	21–50 %	51+ %
AGENTS IN FIRM						
Group Term Life						
Independent Contractor	2	2	1	0	2	2
Employed Licensees	3	3	1	3	4	12
Administrative Staff	5	3	4	5	6	17
Profit Sharing						
Independent Contractor	2	2	3	2	3	7
Employed Licensees	3	2	2	2	2	12
Administrative Staff	4	3	4	3	6	23
Pension Plan						
Independent Contractor	1	1	3	1	0	0
Employed Licensees	2	2	2	2	0	5
Administrative Staff	3	2	5	3	4	10
Health Insurance						
Independent Contractor	19	15	20	24	28	48
Employed Licensees	15	11	13	17	24	48
Administrative Staff	21	14	18	27	39	67
Errors and Omission Insurance						
All Sales Staff	62	45	73	83	88	95

Source: Modified from the National Association of REALTORS® Profile of Real Estate Firms, 1996.

BUYER BROKERAGE

A relatively new area of compensation is buyer brokerage. By mid-1997, there were already over 12,000 REBAC members, many of whom either have the buyer's agent designation or are currently in programs to obtain that designation. A study by Sprint of 232 of their relocating employees found that those who hired buyer's brokers paid an average of 91 percent of the homes' listing price while those who used the more traditional brokerage approach paid an average of 96 percent of the homes' listing price. That is a substantial savings of 5 percent (*Money Magazine,* 1993, 22(4), page 20).

Most believe that buyer brokerage will have an increasing impact on the industry as consumers look for ways to save money on the purchase of a home. Moore sees "most revenue coming in through buyer representation rather than through more traditional practices. The question is, will it happen in three years, five years, or seven years?"

Buyer brokerage may be used more in the future if a certain type of compensation system referred to as "residual shares contract" becomes used. This approach, suggested in a 1995 *Real Estate Review* article by Colwell, Trefzger and Treleven, suggests restructuring the compensation so both the selling broker and the buyer's broker are compensated for their skill in negotiating the purchase price.

The concept works like this. The listing agent and buyer's agent split the percentage of commission on the original listing price of the home according to who did the better job of negotiating the price. A $100,000 home with a 6 percent commission would work like this. If the selling price was $105,000, the selling agent did a better job of negotiating and would receive 5 percent more of the commission on the $100,000 listing price, or $3,150. The buyer's agent would get $2,850. If the selling price was $95,000, the listing agent gets $2,850, and the buyer's agent gets $3,150. Interesting concept. Of course, there are bugs in the system, but this approach is a different way of looking at the transaction and appoaches like this may have some merit in the future.

NEED FOR REWARD SYSTEM PLANS IN THE FUTURE

As we saw, there are quite a few methods to compensate agents. Currently, 91 percent of those methods are percentage commission splits of one form or another (including 100 percent commission plans). The future will require a somewhat different approach if the industry is going to effectively deal with the needs of the consumer and remain the dominant force in residential real estate sales. Three issues will drive compensation or reward systems in the future.

Compensation plans should shift more to a rewards system approach. In the past, the focus has been on the amount of commission the agent receives for his or her services. That is why most of the plans are labeled "compensation plans." This approach rewards entirely on money, one of the broker's scarcest resources. There is a need to focus more on reward systems. Rewards are anything seen as positive or negative by others. Effective brokers will focus primarily on rewards viewed positively by each agent and tailor programs to meet those needs. This approach will include anything (cash related, ego related, etc.) as long as it is cost-effective. In the future, we will see a more comprehensive approach, valuing such things as money, quality of leads referred, types of recognition rewards/opportunities, training bonuses (money toward a training program preferred by the agent and endorsed by the company) and ancillary/affinity relationship opportunities/discounts. Cocks notes that "brokers are starting to realize there is a problem in their company, and after paring down all costs they are now realizing the problem is in the compensation system itself."

Plans in the future will need to be more flexible and better able to meet the needs of the agent, the consumer, and the broker. This flexibility will require compensation from areas other than commissions. Both consumers and brokers believe commission plans are too rich for the agent. Considering the increasing power of the consumer in the residential real estate transaction, the industry needs to adjust before someone enters the marketplace with a better "mousetrap." Bob Kyle succinctly states, "I think there are some ways that we can actually improve services and for a lower cost through greater efficiency. The consumers are going to push and push to get more service for a lower cost, and consumers are the main force behind the structure that will evolve."

There is a need to "think out of the box" and be very creative in how agents price their services to the consumer and how the broker prices his services to the agent. We will start to see a multiple-tier approach. Agents will start to charge the consumer much differently for the services they render. Shopping lists where consumers can check off those services rendered by the agent are an example of this. The consumer can buy one service at a time or a bundle of services. The same approach will work between the broker and the agent. Brokers will begin to offer agents higher commission plans with charge backs for services the broker can offer the agent much more cost-effectively for a fee.

EXAMPLES OF NEWER, MORE PROGRESSIVE PLANS

There are numerous types of plans and approaches to compensation and rewards systems. We just example a few here.

An extremely comprehensive plan developed by Howard Hanna Real Estate in the Pittsburgh, Pennsylvania, area was reported in a 1997 issue of the *Real Estate Broker's Insider.* One specific aspect of the plan is what they call the "Income Advantage Program." This program is open to all agents with $25,000 in real estate commissions and referrals the previous year. Participants receive a check at midmonth as an advance against their commission based on 50 percent of the agents' earnings last year. If they made

$25,000 last year, they would receive a midmonth check of approximately $1,000. At the end of month they would receive the residual of what is owed them depending on their sales that month. "In addition to the financial 'reward' we find this type of system helps motivate agents and eliminates the 'ups' and 'downs' associated with being a real estate agent. Many competitive firms have adopted this program, or at least a part of it, and are using it to reward their agents," states Howard Hanna, president of the company. The company takes a very comprehensive approach to the reward system and rewards agents in numerous other areas as well:

- Selling internal listings with a special weighted commission bonus according to the number of exclusives they obtain
- The health plan agents can choose to use as well as the options of their choosing
- Profit sharing
- Trips to Europe for performance
- Bonuses for top producers

In addition, the company offers nonfinancial rewards. "All agents like to be recognized for their work, and we want to take the opportunity to do that. Recognition can take many different forms here. It doesn't always mean financial types of reward either. It also involves sitting down and writing a personalized card to staff on their birthday. Sales associates are always surprised that the president of a large company actually took the time to sit down and write a note on a birthday card," states Hanna.

- The company web site—this site has external photos of homes, listings, and mortgages with a prequalifier, which helps customers determine if they can afford to purchase the property
- Training is another non-financial reward

- "Fast Start Training Program" on productivity, legal and disclosure issues, how to use technology
- Training courses on mortgages, finance, title, insurance, the importance of one-stop shopping services for the consumer

Although much training is offered, Hanna is not high on using motivational speakers. "Sometimes, we bring in outside speakers, but we find they are much too motivational and they don't focus enough attention on the day-to-day details. If agents need motivation, they should be getting it from sales managers," he states.

The company even has an affinity relationship referred to as Howard Hanna Home Improvement. To bypass the problems experienced by the home improvement companies such as the HFS Century 21 approach that was not effective, their home improvement program offers only certain services such as repairs of roofs, doors, windows, and other accessories, not home expansions.

Keller Williams Real Estate, headquartered in Austin, Texas, was one of the first firms to offer profit-sharing options. Their plan is fully compensation oriented but is rather flexible within the system. Agents get a split up to a certain sales volume, at which point they go to a 100 percent concept for the rest of their transactions within a certain year. In addition, agents receive a certain percentage of profits from a profit-sharing pool that is distributed each month. The hoped-for outcome of this profit-sharing pool is to create more of a team approach within the organization.

A salary concept where agents get salary plus benefits has also been created by an organization called Home Marketplace. The client has the opportunity to choose from a list of services offered by the company and pay for each service. Any service that does not meet the need of the client is fully refundable. Salaried agents, in addition to their salaries, receive insurance, retirement, vacation and a company car.

These three examples by no means exhaust the different types of reward systems that are now being offered. The intent of including them here is to demonstrate that some organizations are trying new programs that are being received positively in the marketplace. The Howard Hanna Real Estate and Keller Williams models have both been in use long enough to say they have been successful. The Home Marketplace approach just began in 1997 and is relatively untested.

ANCILLARY SERVICES AND AFFINITY PROGRAM MOVEMENT

Two recent trends concern the development and use of ancillary services by both agents with their clientele—the home buyer and seller—and brokers with one of their primary clientele—the agent. These services may not be considered compensation plans per se, but they can and will provide added funds to the company, which will allow for more creative and different ways to compensate agents. In some situations ancillary services may be a way for agents to personally generate greater revenues. Ancillary services agents and brokers use with home buyers and sellers include mortgage origination and mortgage insurance. Ancillary services offered by brokers to agents include leads management and certain marketing efforts. Affinity company programs offered to home buyers and sellers include home improvement and satellite television services. Both the ancillary or affinity programs are at the beginning of their use in the industry, but they make so much sense that many see them as having great potential once they have been refined and more effectively marketed.

Dennis Gould, one of the owners of CompensationMasters, makes some very insightful statements about affinity relationships. "If the agent has to lift a finger or if the affinity service may negatively affect the agent's relationship with their client, the home buyer or seller, the sales representative does not get interested. HFS and other organizations try to develop a seamless way to do this, but because it is a relationship business, the sales representatives just get angry especially if it can interfere with that relationship. There is now a move to try to do this without getting the agent in the middle. Brokers are now developing different channels that allow them to bypass the agent. Some brokers are getting leads from new home builders, getting a referral fee, and then handing it off to the agent."

A 1996 Abelson & Company study examined numerous ancillary and affinity relationship opportunities. Seventy-nine RealTRENDS top 250 firms participated in a mail survey. Most of those people responding were firm presidents. Several of the ancillary and affinity opportunities were of great interest to these company presidents. For example, a program to generate leads of buyers and sellers from a mortgage origination company was of interest fairly often 15 percent of the time, of interest very often 23 percent of the time, and always of interest 44 percent of the time, for a total level of interest of 82 percent of the time. See Table 8.3 for more information, ancillary and affinity services examined, as well as the level of interest for each of these.

ISSUES AND TRENDS TO LOOK FOR IN THE FUTURE

The real estate industry has experienced a significant profit squeeze because of some of the past values, philosophies, actual actions and practices. If we are to prepare for the future, we must more effectively deal with these values, philosophies, actions and practices. The following highlights should help prepare us for the future.

TABLE 8.3 Ancillary Services/Affinity Relationships

Percent of Brokers Interested in This Issue

Issue	Never %	Once in a While %	Sometimes %	Fairly Often %	Very Often %	Always %
A leads-generation program providing seller and buyer leads	0	6	11	15	23	45
Discounts for your customers on settlement service costs	10	3	18	9	24	36
Additional revenue generators (e.g., marketing fees from title insurance)	4	4	9	9	24	50
You and your agents receive discounts on goods/services, related to the real estate business, such as						
long distance service	3	9	24	14	18	32
cellular phones/rates	1	8	23	17	17	34
marketing and printing materials	3	9	25	12	14	37
office and agent supplies	3	10	24	10	17	36
computers/software	3	5	21	17	18	36
automobiles	5	12	27	9	15	32

Source: Abelson & Company "Computer Loan Origination Study", 1996.

Values and Philosophies

- The broker has a need and a general desire to attempt to more effectively control his or her destiny. We will see actions such as the use of ancillary services and affinity relationships as well as more profit-maximization approaches.
- There will be a movement to get away from the market share and gross revenue mentality that has helped create the high commission splits and more into a net profit mode.
- Brokers will attempt to develop reward systems that meet the needs of the broker, agent and consumer. They will realize "there are only so many pennies in a dollar. Brokers will allow the agents to pick the plan that allows the broker to be profitable, but meets the needs or style of the agent as well," states Cocks.
- Brokers will need to go to a model where agents have value and are not easily replaceable. This will require the broker to spend more time identifying and affiliating the right agents from the very start. At the same time, they will realize that no one is irreplaceable and not let the top producers overstress their value to the firm.
- Brokers will also affiliate more people from universities and others with potential so the industry will be seen as more professional by the consumer, who will be making value judgments on the worth of the real estate agent's services. Real estate firms may or may not actively recruit on college campuses, but more people who have college degrees will seek out careers in real estate as the professionalism within the industry increases.
- Brokers will need to spend more time managing and less time in direct sales. This will allow them to leverage their time to produce the most profit.
- Brokers will realize they cannot "plug and play" compensation systems and will develop true reward sys-

tems that meet the needs and cultures of their organization, their agents and their target consumer markets.

- Everyone in the industry will need to think more "out of the box" and take chances in how they reward agents. There are substantial changes on the horizon, and the industry is going to need the type of staff that can adapt and change quickly. The changes over the last several years are nothing compared to the changes we will face in the future.

Actions and Practices

To meet all of the above and more, we will need to see the following:

- The use of more ancillary and affinity programs to help meet the financial needs that will arise out of changing compensation programs in the future.
- The use of more fringe benefit programs to foster a higher quality of agent and to use something other than commission dollars to motivate loyalty and longevity of top-producing and other agents.
- We will use objective measurement tools to more efficiently and effectively identify agents with the greatest probability of success so we can more efficiently and effectively prepare staff for the challenges ahead.
- A shift to agents getting smaller commissions per sale, but because of greater efficiency in the office—as well as a shift to ancillary and affinity programs—the agent will make more sales devoting the same amount of time and therefore make as much, if not more, money.
- We will see greater use of buyer brokerage and deal with the pressures this may exert on the compensation systems within the industry.
- We will see greater use of the employee status as relocation companies and other referral organizations attempt to get a greater piece of the commission pie

through nontraditional approaches to the business. We will also see the broker offer more services for a fee to the agent, which will also result in having more paid staff within the industry and a true economies of scale, which will streamline the time and effort agents spend on each transaction.

- We will see more hybrid reward systems that tie together commission and other means of rewards in an attempt to motivate and reward all staff in as efficient a manner as possible. This will help the industry prepare for the invasion of some outside force with a different system that is more efficient than the one we currently use.

The industry has its challenges ahead of it. In order for us to be able to effectively confront reality true reward systems will need to emerge that meet everyone's (broker, agent, consumer, administrator throughout all levels of real estate organizations, ancillary and related organizational staff) needs. Optimists say we will succeed. Cynics say "good luck." What do you say? What will you *do?*

CHAPTER *9*

Is Tech the Ticket to Ride?

"There is nothing in real estate that cannot be recorded, transcribed, databased, transmitted and distributed electronically."

Allen Sabbag, president, Real Estate Group, Meredith Corporation

"There will certainly be successful brokers who will never touch a computer and totally avoid the Web—but their numbers will decline each year."

Peter Miller, consultant and manager, America Online (AOL) Real Estate Desk

The information age dawned upon us in the mid-1970s and was greeted by many as the biggest invention since the Middle Ages. By the early 1980s technology started to make major inroads into business, and the impact of computerization was felt for the first time in real estate. A wave of items, many of which had been invented years before, suddenly surged onto the market. Within less than a decade, the cellular phone, pagers, personal computers, modems and fax were embraced by the business world to such an extent that conducting business today without those innovations is unthinkable.

The second wave of new technology came in the early 1990s when such innovations as compact disks, electronic mail, satellite communication and the Internet became commonplace. Today technology is part of our everyday life, as can be seen by the large percentages of U.S. households using numerous different technology components (see Figure 9.1).

In the real estate industry, practitioners also have more choices today than at any other time in the past, yet they have far fewer than they will have tomorrow. An abundance of choices has created an abundance of confusion. Although many in the real estate industry have learned to accept change, they actually need to aggressively respond to the opportunities it creates. Changes are occurring with ever-increasing speed, and the effect on the real estate industry will be enormous. The impact that technology can and will have is also no longer limited to improving the existing operations but in fundamentally changing the total structure of an industry.

This will result in a total redefinition of many of our existing relationships, what they are worth and what they can achieve in the future. The first thing we need to understand is that large portions of the American economy, including the real estate and mortgage industry, were built on the model of our understanding of the world as it has functioned during what is generally referred to as the Industrial Revolution. The focus of industrialization was effectiveness, that is, the volume of raw output. This led to centralized "massive" infrastructures, large companies, huge governments, labor unions, limitations on information distribution, licensing procedures, etc.

Many industries and professions have evolved and adapted over time. Some resist change, soon to find themselves under siege from an external source. Many times the change was easy; sometimes it was painful. However, with the explosion of technology, change has come swiftly and in some cases almost reengineered whole industries overnight. For example, consider the impact of the compact disk on vinyl records or the impact of the fax on the telex machine.

The genius of technology in the new age is that two people using the exact same tool (e.g., software) can produce

FIGURE 9.1 U.S. Household Technology Use

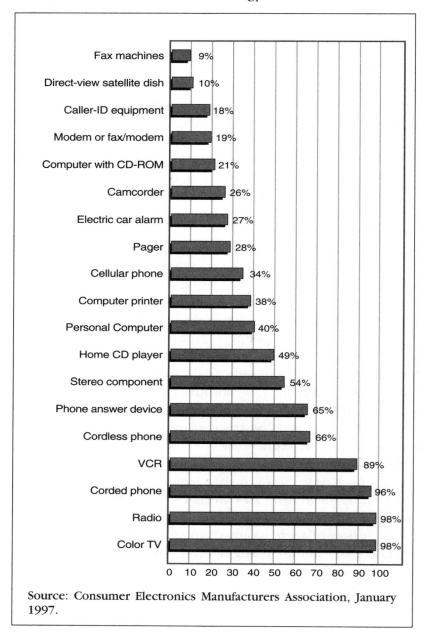

Source: Consumer Electronics Manufacturers Association, January 1997.

dramatically different results in terms of quality, quantity and value in the marketplace. Technology focuses on efficiency, which in turn leads to decentralization and emphasizes knowledge. While technology is revolutionary, it also brings some special problems associated with it. Most people raised during the Industrial Revolution have unflexible paradigms that make it difficult to grasp the benefits that technology will bring.

WILL TECHNOLOGY REALLY CHANGE THE REAL ESTATE INDUSTRY?

For those who haven't noticed it yet, technology has already changed the real estate industry. Just look around at the high number of pagers, cellular phones, fax machines and even Home pages on the Internet. Yet with all that technology used by thousands of individuals, the industry as a whole has failed to truly optimize the power of technology to its own benefit. The industry has embraced it and resisted it, at the same time.

According to an index compiled and published by the Abelson Trends Report, the number one current trend—by almost three to one over the next highest ranking technology trend—is how technology will impact how the real estate industry will run the real estate business in the future. The research indicates that only 40 percent of real estate practitioners effectively use technology today, while 81 percent agree that real estate practitioners will be using technology effectively in the year 2000. The TrendWatch Index (see Table 9.1) ranks a list of technology trends in 1995 according to an index that determines their importance. The same trends are then again ranked in the year 2000, showing which trends are expected to increase or decrease over the next five years.

During the last few years, technology has done something the industry has struggled to do for 10 to 15 years—increase the quality of service and information, and this is just the beginning. It is expected that technology will emerge as the single largest contributor to the way real estate agents interact with their customers. By the year 2000, the information age will be upon us in full blast, and technology will be used to increase the speed of transmission, the accuracy of transmission and the quality of information transmitted. Doing business without computers by the year 2000 will be like doing business without telephones today. According to Dennis Galloway, "Technology is going to create and deliver a lot more than anyone can currently imagine."

One of the largest benefits real estate practitioners will enjoy in the new wave of technology will be mobility. The world is shrinking, business is happening faster and faster and huge sources of information are readily available. The portable computer and the Internet will undoubtedly become the cornerstones of the real estate warrior of the future. Offering inexpensive, quick and effective solutions, the portable computer will be your six-pound support team and the Internet your electronic yellow pages.

"Real estate practitioners must stay technology advanced to stay in the transaction," says David Martin, COO of Real Estate Buyer's Agent Council (REBAC). Real estate practitioners start today by creating a "personal electronic road kit" that tells them where on the Internet they can find all the critical items they might need in the average transaction. Complete information will be a key to their future success.

TABLE 9.1 Technology Trends

	1995		2000	
	Index	**Rank**	**Index**	**Rank**
Technology impacts how we run our real estate business	157	1	156	1
Use of technology increases	57	2	48	3
Firms make greater use of computer systems	41	3	19	9
More agents purchase computers	41	3	16	11
There is an information explosion	37	5	38	4
More people use laptop computers	29	6	27	7
Brokers invest more in computer software	27	7	13	15
Agents effectively use technology	25	8	20	8
Brokers purchase more computers	25	8	5	23
Technology results in more services to customers	24	10	52	2
Changes in MLS technology helps agents	21	11	11	16
Technology results in more services to agents	18	12	15	12
Agents invest more in computer software	16	13	10	17
Technology results in the need for fewer real estate agents	13	14	37	5
Brokers spend more to teach agents to use technology	12	15	8	18
Agents spend more on training to use computers	10	16	17	10
More use of video technology training	9	17	8	18

TABLE 9.1 Technology Trends *(Continued)*

	1995		2000	
	Index	**Rank**	**Index**	**Rank**
Technology results in less need for physical office space	8	18	30	6
Real estate satellite television expands services beyond training	6	19	8	18
Real estate satellite television helps the industry	5	20	14	13
Use of wireless transmission in the field increases	5	20	14	13
Consumers buying homes directly via satellite TV in their homes	5	20	7	21
E-mail used more in real estate	5	20	3	26
Real estate satellite TV impacts training delivery	3	24	2	27
Interconnectedness/ networking of computers increase	2	25	4	25
Wireless transmission across computers occurs	2	25	6	22
Need to use real estate satellite network services increases	1	27	1	28
People use technology to shop interest rates nationally	0	28	5	23

Source: TrendWatch Index, 1996

WHERE DID THE INTERNET BEGIN?

In the early 1960s, the U.S. Department of Defense was seeking a solution to creating a decentralized computer network so that there would be no single point of failure. They appointed a technology company, BBN, to develop what today has become the foundation of the Internet. BBN is also credited as the company that invented the modem, sent the first e-mail and selected the @ symbol.

By the end of the 1960s four different defense sites were connected to the Defense Advanced Research Projects Agency (ARPANet). In the following decade advances in networking protocols led to the creation of the TCP (Transmission Control Protocol) and the IP (Internet Protocol) . In 1987 the National Science Foundation (NSF) used a TCP/IP network to create NSFNet and connect the main computers at various different universities. This led to the opening of the Internet and the beginning of a new revolution.

The Internet exploded in 1994, when the future impact of its existence became so profound that the world engulfed it in awe. To date, no other element of the information age or development of the technology era has amassed so much excitement and support with such vigor and energy. However, as we approach the last few years of the 20th century, the Internet remains as untamed as the Wild West was in the 19th century.

Few people doubt that the Internet will eventually become as common as, say, the cordless telephone. The debate is, however, whether its impact will be that of say, the microwave, the television or the wheel. Will society purely use it as a tool of convenience, will it transform habits and human behavioral patterns or will it totally transform society as a whole? Much of the difficulty in predicting the impact it might have arises from the fact that the Internet is still very much in its infancy and only very limited statistics and trend information is available.

FIGURE 9.2 Current and Estimated Growth of Internet Users in the United States

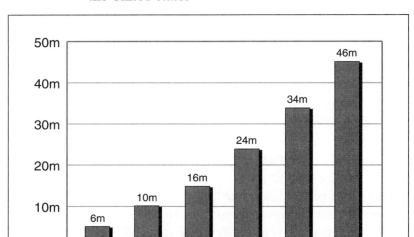

Source: US Digital Research, 1997

In 1996 approximately 33 percent of the Fortune 500 firms reported having a Web site. Toward the end of 1997, the number had rocketed to almost 100 percent. If those statistics are anything to go by, the Internet is booming. Does that mean everyone else is also traveling on the Information Superhighway? No, but the numbers of consumers on the Internet, depending on which report you subscribe to, could be huge (see Figures 9.2 and 9.3).

Another indication of Internet growth is the increase of Uniform Resource Locators (URLs). An URL is like a postal address or phone number for a home page on the Web and is a good indicator of activity. In January 1993 there were 1.3 million URLs. By mid-1997, the number has soared to almost 17 million, rising at about 100,000 a month. Another big driver of the Internet will be the growing use of e-mail. In 1992 some 2 percent of the U.S. population used e-mail, while the number in 1997 grew to approximately 20 percent. Forrester Research, Inc., estimates that the number

FIGURE 9.3 Growth of PCs in Households & Households with Internet Link

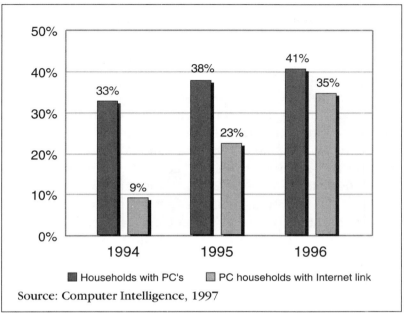

Source: Computer Intelligence, 1997

will continue to grow to approximately 50 percent by the year 2001.

Promises, however, of a cheap, reliable and universal communication have not yet materialized and might be a few years off. There are still many glitches in cyberspace. Security remains a concern, information flow is still relatively slow, many services are not 100 percent reliable and we have not yet reached true real-time capabilities. Understandably, the Internet is still a baby and only starting to mature as a new business technology. With the current rush of people flocking to "the Net," the telephone system is collapsing because it was not designed to handle high data volumes. In August 1996, America Online (AOL) stranded 6 million customers for 19 hours during a blackout. In November 1996, AT&T WorldsNet Service lost e-mail messages sent by 200,000 subscribers. Last summer Pacific Telesis Group had to turn away 16 percent of all calls at its switching center in Silicon Valley. According to many, this is just the beginning of numerous problems all Internet Service Providers (ISPs) can expect to experience.

Is it possible that the restrictions or limitations in the development of a business trend might for the first time actually be the technology and not human acceptance and implementation?

The problems, of course, stem from the many people who due to flat fees, stay connected to the Internet for hours, or even days, thereby dramatically limiting the number of available lines. The local phone companies cannot handle the existing strain, let alone the prediction of 200 million users in the year 2001. Although fibre-optic links—such as the one being built by Quest Commnications—may ease the strain, to correct the current problem and prepare the lines for future users is estimated to cost well over $2 billion and take as long as two to five years to complete.

It would seem, most agree, that the Internet is going to be the communication and marketing tool of the early 2000s. But until then, buckle up—it's going to be a bumpy ride.

THE INTERNET AND REAL ESTATE

The Internet is affecting many different businesses, many in very much the same way. Industries that have traditionally hoarded information, such as the stock exchange, have now seen their information become an open commodity, with very little intrinsic value. For example, only a few years ago Reuters was one of the only ways to obtain shares prices on a regular basis and, as such, subscriptions cost a considerable amount. Today that information is available at basically no cost from a variety of sources. Real estate information, in particular MLS information, is expected to follow this path.

The introduction of the Internet to the mainstream real estate industry started in 1995 at the NAR convention in Atlanta. Initial comments from real estate practitioners varied, with strong comments about the viability of this new innovation. Two years later HFS COO John Snodgrass, who in 1995 had just purchased Century 21 (refer to Chapter 3 for more details on HFS), said, "I was not a technology or Internet fan, I didn't have an open mind—but I've changed. Today the Internet is everywhere and destined to be a major factor in real estate."

Although the number of real estate practitioners using the Internet continues to climb sharply, the real estate industry as a whole has not yet figured out how the Internet will change the way real estate practitioners will work in the future. Concerns are also growing around data ownership as well as meaningful methods of generating real value from a real estate web site.

The largest challenge seems to reside around the real estate data, both the ability to effectively market a house for sale on the web and the ability to effectively draw a large number of consumers to it. The low cost of marketing on the web has created a glut of real estate data—information overload. It is estimated that there are already more than 100 million web sites of which some 3 million reference real estate. If you focus on web sites that actually deal with residential real estate practitioners and homes for sale, the number declines to 100,000. The International Real Estate Digest (IRED), comfortably the largest dirctory of real estate web sites, lists some 15,000 real estate web sites that it has evaluated and currently links to. Even this is still a ridiculously high number of locations, and it is meaningless for a consumer to visit them all.

Boastful marketing claims of the number of "hits" a site receives are largely misleading. These numbers do not really have any meaningful value as they generally reflect the number of pages or listings viewed and do not reflect the number of site visits, let alone the number of unique or serious buyers. Like fishing tales, comparisons have become prone to exaggerated claims of millions and even tens of millions of hits per day, contributing even more to the confusion.

Today, with very few rules and very little order on the Internet, an accurate comparison is difficult. Furthermore, the method of operations differ vastly. Some Internet companies don't warehouse listing information but search other companies files; other Internet companies pluck information from another location, such as MLS companies creating new cyberdatabases within days; and some actually design and manually input the information. Whatever is right or wrong, time and a few lawsuits will probably tell. Irrespective, it is clear that the previously closely guarded MLS information is being set free.

The information is free in cyberspace but, at this stage, still very much lost to the consumer. Only a few real estate practitioners have learned that being on the web does not in any way guarantee success or a high number of consumer trafficers. In fact, only a very select few sites really have meaningful viewership. For example, assume that your company actually does have a few thousand listings. This would qualify your Internet site as one of the largest real estate sites, maybe even in the top 1 percent of all real estate web sites. Being one of the top 1 percent would place you among, say, the top 1,000 sites. That would mean the consumer would still have to wade through 1,000 different real estate sites to view your listings. Not practical at all.

Clearly well-known brands such as Coldwell Banker, Century 21, Better Homes and Gardens, RE/MAX, etc., will have the brand recognition and ongoing marketing budgets to lure certain consumers to their web sites. Due to the very low costs to create and maintain a web site, it is important for most real estate practitioners to have their own web page. However, from the consumer's perspective, it is only an electronic calling card, and consolidation of information will be a requirement before widespread use really can take off. Consumers want simplicity and effectivity. It will be necessary for a majority of houses for sale or for specific types of properties or markets to be available at just a handful of locations.

As a result, the short-term technological race has erupted to see who can gain a large enough cross section of the listings to enjoy critical mass. Many real estate professionals claim that this war is creating so much confusion that it threatens to destroy the very structure that has kept the industry alive the last few decades. A few feel that the number of listings is less signifcant but that it's time to change old antiquated rules and revitalize the industry by introducing significant content and integration of the transaction.

"There is so much information and so many contacts out there, it's often hard to sort through it all," says Jack Peckham, Executive Director of the Real Esate Cyberspace Society. As such, it is difficult to determine the exact quantity of listings on the web. However, using the NAR statistics of approximately 4 million sales per year, and allowing for the average time on market, it is estimated that there are approximately 2.5 million listings on the market on average. Allowing for duplication, it is estimated that the top web providers were hosting about 1.5 million listings on the Internet by end 1997.

Clearly, no single Internet site will be able to monopolize all the real estate information. A handful of web sites will probably end up hosting the majority of real estate listings, have significant content and be able to integrate the different elements of the homebuying process successfully.

Those web sites will focus on different industry needs and probably appeal to different consumer markets.

At this stage it seems that the leading Internet providers for the real estate industry are focused as follows:

- RealSelect (focusing on keeping the Realtor® at the center of the transaction and becoming the national MLS)

- CyberHomes (another strong player in the automation of MLS listings on the Internet)
- US Digital (also known as HomeWeb, focusing on one-stop shopping)
- Homes and Land and Harmon Publishing (focusing on increasing print advertising and Internet advertising)

Pricing, a major issue two years ago, has now almost completely disappeared, with many Internet services being offered to the real estate industry at very low price points. For example, for about $100 a real estate agent could have a home page with all of his or her personal details and qualifications, a picture and e-mail functionality. With little to no money to be made at those levels, many are questioning the longevity and permanency of some Internet providers.

Many agree that ultimately Corporate America will not overlook the fact that the Internet could become the marketing and communication vehicle of the year 2000 by introducing a more effective way to transact with the 3 million home buyers and 4 million sellers every year. Somewhere in the future there is a working model that will generate sufficient volume to attract advertisers to promote their products to the home-buying and home-selling consumers so that the small income from real estate practitioners is insignificant.

The next step will thus be to see which of the Internet providers will create a high enough profile to draw a consistently high number of serious buyers to a real estate site. Jupiter Communications has estimated that the total dollars spent on web advertising is in the early stages of development and could, by the year 2000, reach $5 billion in revenues. How much of this revenue will filter through to the real estate web industry is uncertain.

So by the end of 1997 it is safe to say that the Internet has truly made its impact on real estate and is at this stage in some regards a very large electronic bulletin board. What, is however, apparent is that the Internet is here to stay. It would seem prudent that real estate practitioners should prepare themselves before it is too late.

Gary Buda, of Better Homes and Garden Real Estate Services, says, "To be a web surfer is like being a pilot. You have to log hours to do both before you understand how it works. If you don't, you will crash."

"The key is not to sell through the Internet but use it as a means to access the customer," according to Snodgrass.

NONINDUSTRY INVOLVEMENT

Is there a threat of outside involvement in the real estate industry? Many people, like Jim Sherry, John Tucillo and Karun Khanna, believe the answer is yes.

An obvious candidate, frequently mentioned, is Microsoft—especially after Bill Gates, chairman of the Microsoft Corporation, was quoted in 1996 listing real estate as one of four industries that would be revolutionized by technology. Microsoft has dominated almost every industry or functionality it has become involved in. Let's face it—real estate shouldn't be too tough to revolutionize. There are numerous functions that could be improved through automation.

Today we all know and use such products as Microsoft Windows 95, Microsoft Windows NT, Microsoft Office, Microsoft Word, Microsoft Excel, Microsoft Schedule+, Microsoft Outlook, Microsoft PowerPoint, Microsoft Explorer, etc. Microsoft already has a comprehensive line of products available saving real estate practitioners time, reducing costs, improving marketing, simplifying the process and generally attracting more business. Microsoft Back-Office, Microsoft Automap, etc. are already helping real estate practitioners give consumers better service. So what's next? Microsoft Homehunter, Microsoft Homekit,

Microsoft Mortgage Manager and Microsoft One-Stop Home Shopping. Probably. Yes. Home-in-a-Box. A Microsoft box.

However, it is not an outside force that is truly effecting change in the real estate industry—at least not yet—and neither is it from within the industry itself. The force of change is the *consumer*.

WILL THE CONSUMER CHANGE REAL ESTATE?

Consumers are very important and should not be ignored, yet they are. Many in the real estate industry believe they are taking care of the consumer today, yet all they are doing is an excellent job of managing the status quo. Industry experts will tell you that there are simply too many managers in real estate and not enough leaders. The real estate industry has a severe shortage of decisive, focused leaders. Leaders who will build new organizations that will truly reach out and satisfy the needs of the end user.

Leaders live by the knowledge that "if they build it," customers will come. The first step in building a new industry would be to evaluate consumer trends carefully. (Consumer trends and demographics are discussed in more detail in Chapter 5. In this chapter their impact insofar as it relates to technology is discussed). Modern-day consumers have clearly become more educated and more technology savvy. We already know that the baby boomer generation is maturing, that their shopping style is different, that they are frugal consumers and that they have learned to accept and use technology.

This technology-savvy trend among consumers is also increasing with an even faster pace with the next generation. In a 1997 *USA Today/CNN* poll of seventh-through-twelfth grade students, almost half of them use computers on a daily basis. Teenagers in the survey also selected the

Internet (77 percent) over magazines (22 percent) as their resource preference for school reports. When asked what they could live without, video games (82 percent) and VCRs (49 percent) topped the list, with computers at the bottom of the list. Oddly enough, computers were ranked even better than television.

The home-buying and home-selling public has not yet reached a high enough level of computer literacy to dictate the level of technological skills required by the real estate industry. However, the real estate industry will soon learn to expect a much more demanding and knowledgeable consumer. "Service alone will no longer drive the sale," says Jenny.

MLS INFORMATION—TO SHARE OR NOT TO SHARE; THAT IS THE QUESTION

Many say that the NAR owes its success almost exclusively to its ability, in the past, to concentrate information within a very finite and small group of Industrial Revolution elitists. Therefore, if you wanted that information, you had to buy into its system. A REALTOR® had to buy into the local, state and national associations in order to gain access to the MLS system. Today, all of that is unraveling as processing power is decentralized and moved from the central core to the periphery, from mainframes sitting in 800-plus political-geographical locations nationwide to literally tens of thousands, or even millions of desktops via the World Wide Web. Today the creation of a national digital MLS database not only makes sense, but is relatively easy to create, and RealSelect is well on its way to doing so. Technology and, in particular, the Internet and World Wide Web are transforming and transferring valuable real estate MLS information previously monopolized by organized real estate into a virtually free, unlimited location-neutral service.

The MLS has always been a necessary function in a broker-to-broker environment, but now the MLS business could be changing into a business-to-consumer environment. Does the distribution of real estate information to the consumer change the commercialization of the information? Is that wrong or just a new set of rules? Does the real estate industry still need the traditional MLS organizations anymore?

Raold Marth says, "MLSs will not disappear: They will just convert into natural-market area Intranet." Brian June speculates that we are going to see (that is, if the boards remain on the current path) the elimination of most of the MLS systems as we know them today. He predicts that only a few—say 5 or 10—will survive early into the next century and that they will look totally different from how they do today. John Moore believes that the MLS could become public domain completely while John Tucillo believes MLSs will be a factoid of history within five years.

Meanwhile, power struggles have developed around the ownership of the data, and there is already pending litigation over who is the authorized owner of real estate information. Numerous parties, including real estate practitioners, brokers, tax assessors, appraisers, MLS organizations, local associations and even publishing companies, believe that *they* own or have certain rights to the data. Many real estate practitioners, like Burgdorff, believe that because the seller hires the real estate practitioner to sell the property (and not the MLS company or local association), the information clearly belongs to the real estate practitioner. Others counter that the value is only after aggregation of the data has taken place. Meanwhile, we should not forget the primary reason the concept of multiple listing came to fruition—wider exposure of the property resulting in a quicker sale.

But maybe that struggle is a waste of time too. "For some time now, real estate practitioners have been overly concerned with control and ownership of property data," says

Jim Sherry. "Real estate practitioners were falsely informed that whoever controlled the data controlled the market. What they need control over is the transaction and all its components," he says.

Clearly, the rapid emergence of setting data free, combined with the metamorphosis the Internet has brought to the distribution of data, will probably result in the data becoming public domain. If, or when, this happens, the public will still need some kind of a real estate practitioner to help sift through the large amount of real estate clutter. So the function changes from finding the data to interpreting the data. Additional skills will be required to distinguish between fact and fiction, between information and advertising.

It would seem that the existing MLS model is collapsing.

WHAT IS THE FUTURE FOR REAL ESTATE?

Tucillo draws a comparison between the savings and loan (S&L) industry in the 1980s and the real estate industry in the 1990s when he says, "Dramatic change, maybe even implosion, is a possibility."

Those who believe the industry is on the verge of a total redefinition of what a real estate practitioner will do also say that the balance of power is moving away from the real estate practitioner to a new entity. This move is being made possible by technology and being fueled by the consumer. Similar to the 100 percent concept that allowed RE/MAX to grow from a start-up to one of the most significant real estate companies in the world, so will a few companies emerge and grow into new forces in real estate. Most everyone agrees that within a few years, we will have a more streamlined, lower cost transaction model.

During this time of change, numerous ideas, concepts and/or fads will sprout up everywhere. Many will disappear; some will form the basis or even a catalyst for the imminent fundamental change. For example, some say that the industry could see the development of a "super residential real estate consultant" in the next couple of years. These new-generation superagents could be earning a half million to a million dollars a year and will be almost completely technology driven, integrating much of the latest innovations.

Some cite people like Ralph Roberts, a super real estate practitioner from Michigan, who sold more than 500 homes in 1996, as an example. In an interview with an industry magazine, he said, "I firmly believe that if you use technology wisely, there is an 80 percent chance you'll still be in business five years from now. If you aren't using technology there is an 80 percent chance you'll be out of business." Roberts explains that he actually creates a web site for each and every customer, loading data on moving companies, schools, shopping, transportation, amenities, etc. The buyer can then access his or her own private site to review the information. Using the web, Roberts also browses with the client through all the available listings and applies for and receives approval for a mortgage—all in an hour. Roberts is a wonderful example of a real estate practitioner using technology today to satisfy the consumer of tomorrow.

So are you frustrated that you are not like that or confused about all the new technology? Do you feel as though all the new technology is drowning you? Why, may we ask, are you trying to understand everything? Marth puts it succinctly when he says, "It's not the hardware or the software that's the problem, it's the user."

You must distinguish between the necessity to understand the components of a product and the implementation and benefits thereof. Do you understand all the workings of your car, your telephone or the airplane you fly on? Probably not. Do you need to? No.

Since the beginning of time, we have been surrounded by events, products and people we do not truly understand.

Mysteries are not uncommon and will continue to form the basis of civilization. Forget what computers can or cannot do. Start by using technology to perform those functions they have been designed to do better than you. Do not worry about waiting for the next great computer that can do something faster than an existing machine. All new computers are already faster than the human's ability to type or read.

"Real estate practitioners are not going to disappear, but they are going to have to change," says Sherry. Take his advice and start changing today.

CHAPTER 10

Will the Virtual Transaction Become Reality?

"Buyers will contact only one person in the future—a new type of Buyers Agent—who will take care of the whole transaction, including moving, telephones and even pets."

David Martin, COO of REBAC

"Cyberspace is the most powerful form of networking in the world."

Jack Peckham III, Executive Director of the Real Estate Cyberspace Society

As we approach the next century, we will be entering an era where ideas themselves will become the wealth. Already many examples exist, for instance, Bill Gates, who was able to take his ideas and leverage them into previously unheard-of wealth. In real estate and mortgage banking, the best and the brightest will prove their worth by adding knowledge and value to the processes. Information, in itself (because it cannot be contained) will have less intrinsic value, but optimizing that information will be where all value and wealth is created.

Real estate practitioners, appraisers, mortgage loan originators and title insurers exist, in part because of the inefficiencies of the traditional home-buying process. The protection of information by real estate practitioners and numerous unnecessary legal requirements have, for many years, created a cumbersome and expensive process. The real estate industry generally uses technology to organize and disseminate information. Computers are a "core" or "hub" to that information. Like an airline "hub" moves people, computers act as a "hub" to transfer information about people and their homes from one location to another. The success will be determined by how effectively we make these connections, how quickly we can transfer the information and how consistently we can satisfy our customer in the process.

It would seem that the real estate industry has received a command to create one-stop shopping. The consumer is now demanding more effective service. One of the first real estate processes that automation will streamline is the marrying of the actual home purchase and the home-financing processes. Already identified by both the real estate practitioners and the mortgage lenders as crucial, this pairing has been identified by numerous parties as the first official step toward single entry data.

SINGLE ENTRY REAL ESTATE DATA

Real estate data about the average home-buying process are entered many, many times into numerous different technology systems. According to research undertaken by Interealty, this could be as many as 34 times for a single real estate transaction. Clearly, this number can easily be reduced. The question is, however, just how much of the home-buying process can truly be automated effectively? Currently much of the information is located on separate localized databases, but with the ability of the Internet, the next step will be to link the different datasets and to share the data.

The real estate industry is truly in chaos as a result of being littered with proprietary systems. It would seem that the whole real estate industry was built on separate solutions. Many of the large companies have tried to use different software developers to create unique software applications only to find themselves caught up in an expensive strategy that only gives an advantage for a very short time. Differentiation is not in the product. It is not in the technology per se. It is in the implementation.

Single entry is relatively easy. Technologywise, the solution already exists. Someone has to take the leadership position and come up with the protocols for connectivity, a kind of Electric Data Interface (EDI) standard for real estate. The challenge, of course, is the industry's prior track record of accepting any such standard. Some feel that the National Association of REALTORS® is best suited to determine such a standard, while others argue that it is not part of the NAR's function to enforce a business standard, especially in light of its direct interest in companies like RealSelect.

MORTGAGE PLAYERS AND THE REAL ESTATE INDUSTRY

Financial markets have already undergone substantial change. Since the 1980s, technology has played a huge role in improving the services financial institutions offer. Credit cards, automatic teller machines (ATMs), telephone banking, electronic banking and many new innovations have changed the way most of us view the industry.

The more-traditional banking relationship between bank and customer has substantially changed as a result of all this new electronic commerce. For example, previous one-on-one relationships have largely been replaced with ATM contact. Who today knows the manager of the company holding his or her mortgage? How long will face-to-face contact still be the preferred method of obtaining a mortgage loan? Electronic loan applications, electronic approvals and electronic commitments have been possible for some time and have quietly grown in acceptance.

So, in many regards, electronic commerce is already here. The total homebuying transaction includes the real estate sale and bundled together with the mortgage application there is the potential to offer consumers the beginning of a one stop shop. Most financial and mortgage companies are larger and better funded than real estate companies and, as such, are in a much better position to optimize the bundling of services. As new innovations become commonplace, pricing will come down, the fight will move to controlling the origination source and the lenders will start seeking customers. That could mean that lenders could control the customer, and instead of real estate practitioners recommending the lender, the lender would recommend the real estate practitioner.

This was confirmed by Paul Reid, president of the Mortgage Bankers Association, when he said, "We [the Mortgage Banking Industry] need[s] to find a way to act as the gatekeeper in the homebuying process." At a recent MBA convention, the theme was "See your lender first." It is clear that lenders are determined to get early access to the customer, creating brand awareness, creating loyal customers and mining the database for cross-selling. Although sometimes slow in implementation, financial institutions have demonstrated that they are willing and able to embrace hi-touch and hi-tech and also willing to replace traditional approaches for new options.

Has the real estate industry retaliated through real estate giant HFS? (Chapter 3 discusses HFS and its huge impact on the real estate and mortgage industries). "The mortgage industry is horrible," says John Snodgrass. "It is a complex process and it should not be. HFS intends to make a significant improvement to the mortgage process," he adds. These are no idle claims. With the recent acquisition of PHH Inc. together with the earlier acquisition of The Home Mortgage Network (THMN), HFS is already one of the largest leaders in the nation and is the first group to have sufficient market share in both industries to be able to implement a meaningful program.

So while the playing field is being prepared for the battle over who gets to the consumer first, the homebuying procedure will hopefully continue to improve. The transaction approval time should continue to come down significantly, from days to hours, or even minutes, and closings could take place within days. Documentation should become easier to complete and meaningful preapproval or even instant loan commitments should be available in the not-too-distant future.

THE MORTGAGE MARKET OF TOMORROW

Both the primary and secondary mortgage lending markets, however, face a much larger challenge than the growing involvement from real estate practitioners. As new technology opens new avenues of increased efficiency, the secondary mortgage market seems to be poised to bypass the primary lenders and real estate practitioners to become the point of first and, maybe, only contact.

Both Freddie Mac and Fannie Mae are making substantial profits from the mortgage industry. They realize that they, although indirectly, already control the mortgage market. Although their current charter does allow direct access, at this stage they can require players to follow their standards and new technology innovations. Innovations such as the Automated Loan Prospector from Freddie Mac and the Desktop Originator and the Underwriter from Fannie Mae are already available. These personal computer–based software programs organize borrower information, qualify the borrower for the loan, perform the underwriting tasks and then prepare the necessary documentation. One has to wonder whether they need the primary market and whether it is just a question of time before they go directly to the consumer.

Computerized loan origination seems to have been around for ages and has in many areas met with limited success. However, that was before the rapid growth of the Internet. Repackaged and restructured electronic mortgage application and processing through the Internet and with the assistance of videoconferencing is finding wider acceptance. The process is further improved with the availability of electronic credit approvals, document transfers and relaxed previously stringent appraisal requirements.

An interesting recent development is the formation of digital banks; that is, banks that have no public or retail facilities but live in the cyberworld of the Internet. With such low overhead, digital banks can compete very aggressively with traditional banking structures, thereby reducing rates.

As we move toward the seamless transaction, with information gathered from one remote location and the transaction processed from multiple locations simultaneously, it will become increasingly more important to improve the security of the Net. There seems to be a vast consumer concern about the insecurity of technology and in particular the Internet. Brian June comments that existing security measures are much better than they are given credit for and that he is not aware of a consumer that has lost a dime as a result of the Internet. Based on current development paths over the next 12 to 24 months, June expects to see "bulletproof" encryption techniques develop that will facilitate the next development stage in the move toward one-stop shopping for homes.

More Innovations Toward One-Stop Shopping

The real estate industry will experience the development of many new innovations introduced by the emerging growth of the Internet. Some interesting ones expected to have an impact on the home-buying process are listed below.

However, it is not their introduction that has, in the past, made the impact on the industry but rather the industry's acceptance and implementation thereof. Real estate practitioners are renowned for resisting change, and many valid innovations were previously lost. This time around, things might be a bit different for the following two reasons:

1. The majority of the innovations are Internet driven. And, as such, they are relatively cheap and easy to apply and introduce over a large national basis in a relatively short time frame. Previously unheard of products could therefore become commonplace in a matter of months.

2. An increasing number of nontraditional players are becoming involved with or evaluating their involvement in the home-buying process. This would dictate that real estate practitioners should not expect traditional solutions or approaches. Nonindustry players might accept new innovations, whether those innovations make sense to existing structures or not.

Many solutions, resources and sets of information that are already available today have gone almost unnoticed by traditional real estate practitioners. They include such items as tax information, county courthouse records, environmental reports, flood certificates, neighborhood maps, floor plans, etc. "Almost everything, but smelling the cat, can be done electronically today," says Gary Buda, "and even that will be solved one day. Virtual home tours are not far away," he warns.

Interactive Kiosks

Ever since the first ATMs crept into our lives in the early 1980s, consumers worldwide took their first step toward electronic banking. Today those same machines are no longer just a means of getting cash fast, but they also are being used as convenient information sources. With the latest technology, these machines are now turning into marketing showpieces, ticket-vending outlets and even real estate information centers.

Traditionally the machines operated on a resident CD-ROM database; however, recently private Intranet sites have become an effective way to update the data. With the continued growth of hi-touch technology like touch screens, voice and speech recognition, video applications and interactive software, these machines will take on a whole new life in the not-too-distant future.

Some market analysts are predicting that kiosks using these machines will prove successful in industries where salespeople are considered "pushy" or where consumers have a higher need for information prior to making a decision. Although there is agreement that a machine will not replace the real estate agent, it could possibly become a convenient method for consumers to initiate involvement or satisfy a need for more information before actually contacting a real estate practitioner.

Speech Recognition and Holography

The computer of today is indeed several hundred times more powerful than the best mainframes, of a few years ago. When you start approaching the kind of speeds that are becoming readily available today, society starts to see the advent of new technologies, for example, real-time, unique speech recognition. This means that it will be possible in the foreseeable future for computers to react to our voices, thereby adding tremendous security to the computer systems and greater flexibility to our computer use. It would be true "humanlike" speech that has very little pausing and where the voice sounds very natural, much like a human being.

Another technology, holography, although much further away, raises many interesting possibilities. Large (perhaps ten-feet wide and five-feet to six-feet tall) thin-screen projection units, only 1½ inches thick, using holographic techniques will give us true three-dimensional effects unlike anything we know today.

Similar to the holodecks in the television series "Star Trek," holography will allow customers to do a virtual walk-through of homes almost so real that their brains will not be able to tell the difference.

Some say this will be created through the advent of new "cyber real estate practitioners." What cannot be looked at with a live "view cam" will be computer generated, projected in three-dimensional images and, in effect, be so real that a person will not be able to distinguish between the house and the holography. You would be able to move walls around, rearrange furniture, redo landscaping or change colors of paint on walls. In essence, you could change everything about the home in order to determine what it might look like and basically design your own home "virtually" walking around and "commanding" your house to "be."

Narrow casting (i.e., point-to-point transmissions from that camera to a satellite uplink to a web) will enable television to take people from any point in the world and walk them through a property for sale. Few people believe this is possible, yet some are predicting a very small, highly accurate videocamera to be mounted on a real estate practitioner's shoulder. That, in conjunction with narrow casting, will allow a real estate practitioner in California to "walk" the homebuyer through neighborhoods, shopping centers, streets, etc. This will make "virtual walk-through" of homes a reality.

It is expected that this could be available in the next ten years. Therefore, there will be no real reason for people to buy a home "unseen." As stated above, the brain will not be able to distinguish the difference. Thus, we will see homes purchased "sight unseen" from thousands of miles away subject only to a final inspection where the person will physically go there and make the distinction between the virtual world and the real world.

CYBERMONEY

So if you might buy your house without actually visiting the property, why should it be necessary to go somewhere to pay for it? As these futuristic markets expand into cyberspace, so will a growing need develop for some form of currency in cyberspace—something as easy as cash, as effective as checks and as universal as credit cards. Electronic commerce jumped into top gear in 1994 when numerous companies, such as CyberCash, First Virtual and DigiCash, devised some of the first ways for the consumer to pay for purchases via the Internet.

It is still, however, early. With the confusion on the web, finding something to buy is not yet a pleasant experience. According to an Internet demographic study undertaken by Nielsen Media Research in spring 1997, only 5.6 million people (or 15 percent of the people on the World Wide Web) have already concluded a purchase through the web. Current limitations seem to be the current development of virtual malls. Designed on traditional lines, these malls, which have focused on selling hard goods, have met with consumer resistance, thus keeping electronic purchasing down to only around a half a billion dollars in 1996. Furthermore, the biggest challenge for the growth of cybermoney will probably be the existing traditional money instruments. There is not really anything wrong with them. Especially with the realignment of credit cards to support the ever-increasing smaller transaction, cybermoney might be just a bit further in the future.

However, whatever or whenever the monetary instrument of the future will be, don't underestimate the potential extent of retail purchasing on the Internet. If big business is anything to go by, this number will be rising sharply. American Express Travel is currently selling more than $1 million of air tickets over the Internet every day, Dell Computers is selling more than $1 million of PCs a day and large network equipment–maker Cisco is selling its products over the Internet at a rate of $1 billion a year.

Current development trends dictate that we will see the emergence of true cybermoney–money not backed by a central government or a central bank and perhaps under-written by private enterprise, much like the Industrial Revo-lution American Express did with traveler's checks. It will not exist anywhere except in cyberspace, but it will be accepted anywhere as legal tender. It will have additional security: unlike our paper money today, cybermoney will not be subject to rapid depreciation in value due to infla-tion and uncontrolled money printing by governments.

VIRTUAL DIGITAL AGENTS

An interesting development predicted for the foreseeable future is the advent of Virtual Digital Agents (VDA) on the web. VDAs are intelligent autonomous agents that will exist by your creation and act as your "digital slave" on the Inter-net. A VDA will cruise the Internet on your behalf, follow your commands, and search for your requests until it satis-fies your needs and is ready to shop on your behalf.

Brian June believes that homebuyers will in the future have their own VDAs, their own personal avatars and their own personal digital real estate practitioners who will search the world over (regardless on what server the infor-mation resides) and look for the requirements of their dream homes.

When this VDA finds your dream home, it will report back to you on your television, or on your personal computer, or notebook, etc., whether you are flying in an airplane or in the middle of the jungle, that it has found your dream home. This could take minutes, days or might actually be a permanent, ongoing function.

At that point your VDA will deliver—together with the details of your home—all the tax information, construction information, room dimensions, school and shopping information, etc., it has researched for you. Your VDA will be based on your personal criteria and will determine the anticipated quality of life in the new area, evaluate the listing price, do the necessary market analysis, create a relative value index and make recommendations regarding the purchase. Your VDA will take over many of the painful functions currently associated with search and data retrieval and package customized information to your personal requirements.

CONCLUSION: SUCCESS IN THE FUTURE

Most agree that one-stop shopping is a consumer need. Many agree that the Internet is the vehicle that will revolutionize and streamline the home-buying process. We are starting to realize that integration of the different processes and the introduction of a simplified and paperless transaction will save the consumer days and could, in the end, result in a savings of thousands of dollars on each real estate transaction.

It would seem that the real estate industry has taken the plunge and is more than just preparing for the electrification process—it is actually effecting the necessary change. According to Lyle Fuller, vice president of Interactive Networking for Prudential Real Estate Affiliates (PREA), "Our ultimate goal is to create a totally paperless transaction for buying a home. We're closer than you may think."

Maybe the dream of a pleasant, quick and easy home-buying process is not that far away after all.

CHAPTER *11*

Answers for the Next Millennium

Question 1: To what extent will technology influence or alter the way the real estate brokerage business is conducted?

Swanepoel: It is time for the real estate industry to understand that technology is not a destination—it's a journey. Technology is not an enemy—it's a tool. The real estate industry is in a 10 year phenomenon. I would even suggest that technology is the single biggest change catalyst the real estate industry has or will experience in the future.

The home-buying and/or home-selling process has already been and will in the coming years be affected by technology innovations in a dramatic way. Technology will improve market efficiency and the consumer's understanding of the traditional home-buying and/or home-selling process.

Technology and, in particular, the Internet and World Wide Web are transforming and transferring valuable real estate information previously monopolized by organized real estate into a virtually free, unlimited, location-neutral service.

Technology brings efficiency, reliability, flexibility and speed. In a word—value. With open architecture on the Internet, it is now becoming possible to connect the whole transaction and settlement process into one integrated, transparent, paperless transaction. One-stop shopping for real estate can now become a reality.

Dooley: It may not be quite the difference between night and day, but it will be at least the difference between dawn and high noon. As one real estate expert put it, "There will still be real estate agents who do not use technology in their businesses. They will be called 'failures.'" It may well be that the real estate sales agent's mode of operation will be drastically impacted by technology. The computer and other advancements can do in seconds what might take an agent hours to accomplish. Moreover, there is a strong school of thought that believes the very role of "sales agent" will be altered and replaced by "buyer's agent" as representative of the task that most agents will be undertaking in the future.

Abelson: Technology will increase the speed of the real estate transaction, increase the availability of information and improve the efficiency/effectiveness of the entire real estate transaction. This will occur in the entire "servicing channel" from agent behaviors, to broker behaviors, to administrative services, to the associations/organizations that serve the industry.

All members of this servicing channel will do best if they (1) keep their clientele aware of the information/data available, (2) help take that information and transform it into knowledge that their clientele can understand and use, and then (3) share their wisdom or insight as they help their clientele be at the cutting edge in their marketplace.

Agents will have tremendous opportunities to use technology to service the consumer. It will be important that agents have all the latest technology available for their use and make this technology available for their clientele. We have done prelisting qualifications and financial qualifying of buyers to see how much they can afford to spend to buy a home. We now need to add to these a "technology audit" to (1) assess the technological savvy of the clientele, (2) offer to use with them the exact technology they want to have access to or use at the level they want it and (3) offer it to them when they want it. Web pages, e-mail, fax-back information, talking voice mail, talking yard signs, graphic presentations, and any other technological communication mechanism should be available for use with the clientele. But be careful not to intimidate your clientele with your technology. Make sure you present to them the options in a relaxing way and give them the services and servicing alternatives they feel comfortable with, not what you feel comfortable with.

Question 2: What role will HFS play in the real estate brokerage industry and what influences will it have on the industry?

Dooley: Well, its influence is already overwhelming. Whatever course other brokers may be following, it has been modified or altered since August 1995 when HFS first appeared on the real estate scene. HFS may not be "writing the rules" for the real estate industry, as former Century 21 President Bob Pittman said it would, but it surely is blazing the trail and setting the course for the future of the industry. Can it continue to do so? It depends much on the intent of its erstwhile chairman, Henry Silverman. Forthright in his dealings with the press and public, Silverman has always maintained that his job as chairman was to enhance shareholder value. If real estate and related fields of endeavor enable him to achieve this goal, he will continue to pursue them with vigor.

Swanepoel: I do not believe HFS is focusing on the role of industry leader, neither do they desire to necessarily rewrite the rules of the industry. HFS is focused on growing their company by leveraging new business for its subsidiaries/franchisees and optimizing opportunities as the gatekeeper of leads and intercompany transactions. Don't misinterpret focus with impact. HFS will obviously have a significant impact and will in the short term be a trendsetter due to the large market share it controls in the real estate industry. HFS will be a leader in expanding the services offered by real estate practitioners to the consumer and in integrating the different components of the transaction more effectively. If someone will be able to implement one-stop shopping nationwide at the real estate practitioner level today, my money would be on HFS.

Abelson: I am not convinced HFS is here to stay. If I am correct, look for them to start exiting by the year 2000.

If they are here to stay, I see two entirely different ways they will influence the industry. First, they will be a threat to other current real estate organizations. With a current market share of about 25 percent and growing through acquisitions and mergers, their programs can impact any and every market. Their affinity relationships will continue to grow, which may or may not affect others as HFS tries to control more aspects of the transaction. They are a very aggressive player and have the resources to do just about anything they set their mind to do.

I also see HFS as an ally and see their actions giving others an opportunity in the industry. They will keep the industry off balance and keep the competitive juices flowing. They will be friendly competition in that their delivery of services paradigm is very similar to the current industry paradigm. If (or should I say *when*) others enter the industry with a different delivery paradigm, HFS will initially fight the new paradigm just like every other real estate company (unless it is they who deliver the change or they buy up the organization who delivers the change). That will give the rest of the industry, along with HFS, the opportunity to fight and prepare to do battle with the new paradigm. Then, it will be everyone for himself or herself as organizations either die or adapt as quickly as possible to deal with the paradigm shift.

Question 3: Will other corporate giants enter the realm of residential real estate brokerage?

Swanepoel: Most certainly, it is only a question of when. My guess would be that by the year 2000 at least one or two Fortune 500 companies will have expanded their reach into the real estate industry. Most likely candidates will be mortgage, title and technology companies. This does not mean that they will necessarily buy real estate brokerages like HFS, but they could get involved by purchasing industry-related companies involved in the home-buying process and then change the rules.

Abelson: No and yes. First the no. I do not see any other corporate giant coming into the industry and fighting with HFS for market share. With more than 25 percent market share and growing, there would not be enough other players around who wanted to sell to allow a new corporate giant "player" to grow fast enough to compete with HFS. HFS would react very quickly and buy up as many companies as possible to keep the new corporate giant's market share and critical mass too small to do much damage. Of course, some corporate giant could come in and buy HFS and either change things or continue on the path HFS was working on, whatever that happens to be at the time. This is a real possibility, because you will remember from my answer to question 2 that I am not convinced HFS is in this for the long run.

Now the yes. I expect another corporate giant to enter the industry. But this new major player will come into the industry with another major paradigm shift, just like HFS did a couple years ago. They will attempt to capture HFS's and everyone else's market shares. Beware of organizations like

Microsoft; some large financial institution, such as a mortgage banking firm or collective; a large communication company; or a large insurance company. Any of these could enter with a new paradigm, especially a technologically advanced one, and blow everyone out of the water.

Dooley: Could be, especially if HFS continues to exhibit financial success in the field. The likelihood is that any future giant entering the real estate field probably will be dissimilar from HFS in that it will not be principally a franchisor of service industries but rather a communications-and-technology based enterprise that will seek to deploy new methods and methodology to totally change the manner in which real estate transactions are accomplished.

Question 4: How are the large megabrokers likely to change in the coming decade?

Abelson: I see this very likely in two possible directions. First, some megabrokers may start their own franchise. This is already occurring in several markets. Those megabrokers with a strong "brand" name have started to franchise with varying levels of success. Second, I see some groups of companies, such as the Realty Alliance and the Vision, considering starting "national" franchises. They will use the strength of the regional large independent "brand" name(s) in that market. They will also use the synergies of these large coalitions of megabrokers to develop systems that they use personally in their marketplaces and share their most effective systems with megabrokers in other marketplaces. Why should each megabroker "recreate the wheel" when large groups of megabrokers can create a common wheel they can each use and modify in their local markets? Instead of "Franchise—Company Name" we may start to see "Megabroker Coalition Name—Local Regional Broker Name."

Swanepoel: The major independents will undergo substantial change on a variety of levels. Many will disappear as they are purchased by or incorporated into the national franchises; others will themselves buy other large independents in an effort to compete with the national franchisees; and some will utilize franchising themselves as a method for expansion. These real estate companies are highly entrepreneurial, progressive, flexible and can change direction fairly easily. The largest problem they face is the general lack of second-tier management as well as an effective succession plan when current ownership/leadership retires.

Dooley: Only to the extent of "filling in" geographic voids in their market sectors. There is a greater likelihood that they will either merge with or blend certain operations with other megabrokers.

Question 5: Will REALTORS® continue to be the central focal point of the real estate transaction?

Dooley: Yes, the odds favor it because REALTORS® have such a lead on any "opposing forces;" however, the deployment of financial and technological resources can close the gap quite rapidly. Still, we favor the REALTOR® as continuing to be the center point of the transaction, albeit a different style of transaction.

Swanepoel: For the next couple of years, yes, but real estate practitioners are rapidly losing their control over the home-buying process. Technology will replace people that no longer add real value. Although I believe the real estate practitioner will remain an important participant in the home-buying process, the real value will be with the party who can best manage the information, integrate the services and give meaningful value to the consumer. I am of the opinion that the most likely candidate for that role is the financial services industry.

Abelson: Over the next three to five years the answer is absolutely yes. The chances of a major paradigm shift that the consumer will accept in that period of time is relatively low. After that period of time anything can happen.

This is good news for the real estate practitioner. It means as long as the practitioner does business as it has evolved to be in 1997 things should be OK. By the year 2000 expect to make some major changes in the way you do business if you still want to be in business after that point. Technology will continue to increase the speed of everything and make it more costly to stay up-to-date on the latest changes. Expect the biggest changes over the next three to five years—especially in how the broker changes the way business is done. We are entering a period of time when technology is going to impact how the office is managed in a very constructive way. Those who use these advancements will have more efficient, effective and profitable companies.

Question 6: Will real estate brokerage be a profitable enterprise? For brokers/owners/sales agents?

Swanepoel: It will always be profitable for some. However, by the early years of the next decade many revenue streams will change, existing ones will decline and new ones will appear. For progressive-thinking brokers, the future is brighter than it has been for a long time. For those stuck in the paradigms of the 1980s, I would recommend they start seeking alternative career opportunities.

Dooley: Barring a major economic decline throughout the nation, the answer is yes—extremely so for those who are still in the business five or ten years from now. Their numbers will be fewer; their expertise and sophistication will be greater. Their margin per transaction may be considerably less than it is now, but they will command large market shares and will have additional profit streams from activities ancillary to the home sale that, in many instances, will outweigh what they will realize from straight brokerage. Another noticeable trend in this area is that brokers/owners are aggressively pursuing means of readjusting the split revenue received from clients to favor them rather than their agents.

Abelson: Again, my answer is yes and no. I hope you will be on the yes side. Brokers can be profitable, but they will have to adapt to changes and adapt quickly. A big impact will be the reward system and how brokers react to changes in the reward system. The agent, the consumer and the brokerage company will need to all experience rewards. Brokers, in particular, have not shared equitably regarding financial reward. This will have to change. See Chapter 8 about compensation-versus-reward systems for insights on how this can change. Also of importance is technology and how brokers will use it to increase efficiency and effectiveness. As a broker, I would keep my eye on the Realty Alliance companies. This organization is a sleeping giant and is preparing to awake and start walking around and pilfering everything in sight.

Brokerages may *not* be profitable in the future. Data to date show that anywhere from 25 percent to 50 percent of current brokerages are not profitable, and these are good economic times for real estate. What happens when there are some lean years? Watch out for even more mergers and acquisitions.

The answer for agents' profitability is also yes and no. The answer is yes for those agents who adapt. There has always been a minority of agents at the top who are successful. Over the last 10 to 15 years, we have seen this minority shrink further. Agents with systems that work for them will do well. These agents will increase the "barriers of entry" for everyone else. They will keep on increasing the costs to enter because they are already up to speed on the latest and most applicable technology (this costs money) and the amount of expertise (this costs money and takes time) needed to enter the industry or local marketplace. They will continue increasing the amount and speed of change making it that much more difficult to enter the business and be competitive with them.

Question 7:   Will the current commission arrangements continue to be the principal method that

consumers use to compensate real estate firms for services rendered?

Abelson: In the short term, over the next two to three years, the answer is primarily yes. We will see a more programmatic approach to developing compensation and reward systems. Organizations such as CompensationMaster will be in tremendous demand because of their ability to develop plans that are more profitable for brokers and very acceptable to agents.

Dooley: Certainly not as the exclusive or even dominant method of compensation. For one, it is generally regarded as too expensive. In Chapter 6, we quote a well-known real estate expert as saying, "Real estate brokerage is not brain surgery, but we expect to be paid like brain surgeons." That practice will stop if for no other reason than competition will force changes. That may be straight price competition, with the 6 percent or 7 percent commission rate severely discounted or with flat fee arrangements replacing the percentage commission. Or it may be that the "menu pricing" arrangement that has received lots of talk but little action during the 1980s and 1990s may take hold, in the 2000s.

Swanepoel: By the year 2000, most certainly. In the next three years, there will be only minor change—most likely a slight decline in overall commission percentages as consumers, technology and outside interests exert pressure. Charging a specific amount for no specific service is no longer acceptable. Looking ten years ahead, there will be many new structures. Many existing services today could disappear, become free or be available at only a nominal cost. New services will develop and will most likely be menu driven. I would suspect that more salespeople will be on staff rather than independent contractors and remuneration will shift more toward salary with incentives rather than straight commission.

Over the next several years start looking for a shift away from the straight commission method to more of a hybrid method where some of the fees are commission (obviously lower), while other fees are for services offered by the agent and accepted by the consumer. The consumer has started to demand lower commission rates. I believe that the broker and agent do not have the discipline to persuade the consumer that their services are worth the current commission rate of primarily 5 to 7 percent. I personally believe the services rendered are worth the price, but persuading the consumer will take a programmatic approach that most agents will not be willing to do.

We will start to see brokers and agents trying to sell all types of ancillary services directly and indirectly related to the real estate transaction. This will happen as a way to compensate for the decrease in revenue from the traditional commission approach. Also expect to see agents more efficiently using their time as brokers bring more systems in-house through technology that will allow for more effective and efficient use of the agent's time. Agents will be asked to pay for these services if they want to use them, but agents will be able to make more money overall because they will have the time to meet the needs of more consumers and have many more transactions.

Question 8: Will the 100 percent commission concept of compensating agents continue to be viable?

Dooley: I think so, because, in essence, they are folks in business for themselves. It may well be that the rush to counter RE/MAX that occasioned so many other firms to offer their versions of 100 percent plans may be over, but within specialized organizations like RE/MAX, and especially there, I continue to see successful operations structured along the 100 percent lines.

Swanepoel: I believe that the 100 percent concept has lost its positioning as an unique way to compensate real estate agents. Not only have commission arrangements become blurred, but will the change in the services and format of agency alter compensation structures so that this method of compensation is no longer as important as it was 15 years ago. Large 100 percent based companies like RE/MAX, however, will still grow. Not as a result of the 100 percent concept per se, but if they are able to utilize the large number of quality agents the company has brought together under one company. The question is, instead, who will successfully introduce the new real estate practitioner required for the industry emerging?

Abelson: My friends Jes at RE/MAX and Rich at Realty Executives are both going to love my answer. *Absolutely!* I do not see why not. (I love the short answers. I hope you do too.)

Question 9: What effect will buyer representation have on the industry as a whole?

Swanepoel: There is in the end really only one customer. Not the franchisee, not the agent, not the seller, but the buyer. Therefore I believe that buyer agency will have a dramatic impact on the real estate industry. The 1970s adage of "He who controls the listing, controls the transaction" is no longer valid. Consumerism has reversed the roles. Today "He who controls the buyer, controls the transaction." I believe buyer agency will be one of the fastest growing trends in the next couple of years, possibly even bigger than technology on the short term. Watch organizations like the Real Estate Buyer Agency Council (REBAC) outperform and outgrow most other associations during the next couple of years.

Abelson: Buyer representation has had an increasing impact ever since it began having any impact on the industry in the early to mid-1980s. With over 12,000 buyer representatives just in REBAC, their numbers and impact will grow further.

There is both good and bad news regarding the effect of buyer representation. It depends on where you sit. Buyer representation will slowly decrease the price of properties. It will increase industry efficiency and effectiveness and therefore make the industry as a whole stronger. This in itself will help protect the industry from itself and the invasion of an outsider, unless this outside invader enters with a new technology or paradigm. Buyer representation should keep all of us on our toes. There may be the need to do a better job explaining the concept to the consumer so we don't get too distracted with lawsuits. There is even a new way to compensate both the buyer representative and the listing agent so each is rewarded for their efforts at best negotiating for their client. Read in Chapter 8 about the "residual shares contract" to compensate the buyer and listing representatives.

Dooley: By the middle of the first decade of the 21st century, there will be an agent representing the buyer and a separate agent representing the seller in virtually every real estate transaction. They may well be from the same office, although that practice of disclosed dual agency or "designated" agency may be obliterated by future court decisions.

Question 10: Will the consumer's use of real estate practitioners increase, decline or remain stable?

Abelson: As long as the current paradigm remains intact there will be a need for the real estate practitioner. There is always a need for the help of an information expert. With the variety of information currently available, the amount of that information, and the speed at which the information enters and changes increasing daily, the real estate practitioner who is perceived as an expert of this information will always be in need. The practitioner just needs to keep ahead of the rest of the competition on the information curve. Why are you reading this? I hope it is because you believe we are giving you power through the expertise the three of us have on the industry. Experts will always be in demand.

Dooley: I think it will increase because of the following reasons: (1) the incessant time demands that most people are confronted with, (2) the growing trend toward the recognition of areas of specialization and the favorable consumer use of specialists and (3) the fact that successful real estate operators of the future will centralize all of the functions connected with the real estate transaction.

Swanepoel: Although there will be little or no notice-able difference in the next few years, expect a decline on the long term. As an industry the time has come to change. Fueled by consumer demand, unlimited access to information and outside players investigating the real estate industry, it would be prudent now to do an introspection of the way the home-buying process should be conducted in the future.

The answer lies in a fundamental redesign to the entire business process. Maybe not by the year 2000 but soon thereafter. If we do not, death of the traditional real estate practitioner might be slow, but it will be certain. Fortunately, I believe that the real estate industry, although sometimes slow, is dynamic and will make certain changes. Real estate practitioners won't die, but change they will.

Question 11:   Is the consumer really buying into the idea of "virtual reality" as it affects the real estate industry?

Abelson: Absolutely! This is occurring just like it occurs with any new technology or change. There are those people who feel comfortable with new and different things who "buy into" the new approach. As this happens, the new approach improves and becomes more effective/efficient. More and more people "buy in" as the new technology improves, and others see more and more people using it. How long will it take before "virtual reality real estate" really hits and affects everyone? It will take a number of years for the impact of this new approach to have any observable impact. Now is the time to get involved in this approach before others master how to use it and leave you wondering what happened.

Dooley: Not very much right now, but that will change as technological sophistication becomes an "actual" rather than a "virtual" reality throughout large segments of the population.

Swanepoel: If you think electronic commerce is just another buzzword, think again. Technology is creating a new kind of human being, a new kind of consumer. It might be a couple of years away, and it might only really come into full force with the next generation of consumers, but virtual reality is real.

Question 12:   In the true sense of the word, is real estate likely to be more or less a profession by the year 2010?

Swanepoel: The real estate industry has been in awe for a long time with the desire to be a profession. If your perception of a *profession* is the same as lawyers' and doctors', then the real estate industry will never be a profession. If your definition is that of licensing, education and ethical standards, then the real estate industry is already a profession. I believe it is immaterial in any event. With the changes that technology is bringing, real estate practitioners will become more like advisers and facilitators, helping guide consumers, mainly buyers, through the clutter of information and confusion of the home-buying process.

Dooley: Well, what is the "true sense of the word" when it comes to *profession*. If it means an accepted level of collegiate or postcollegiate training, probably not. If it means a high level of skill and talent, then absolutely yes. It's largely a matter of semantics anyway. More and more, the terms *professional* and *craftsperson* are used interchangeably, and perhaps they should be.

Abelson: By the year 2010 the real estate vendor will be extremely professional. This will be true whether that vendor is the real estate agent and broker as occurs in the current paradigm or the real estate transaction occurs through a totally different paradigm. The consumer is having more impact, and real estate information is becoming more easily obtained and better organized. Real estate sales that meet future consumer needs will require effective and efficient management of the real estate transaction. This will require a totally mechanical system or a system that includes a very knowledgeable and respected professional who knows how to manage the technology and people within it. I think it's the latter.

Question 13: If the trends toward universal reciprocity of real estate license recognition between states continues, will there ultimately be federal licensing of real estate agents?

Dooley: Possibly, but more likely the situation will be treated as driver's licenses are now. If an individual is licensed in one state, it will be assumed he or she knows how to operate in another state. However, if the licensee violates a law, he or she will face the consequences imposed by the state in which the violation occurred.

Abelson: *No!* Ownership of real estate is a very personal thing, and people feel their situations are unique. The cultures and needs of the states are different enough that local legislatures will resist national licensing. Another industry has numerous commonalities of needs and has a situation similar to real estate in some regards—the utilities industry. Both industries have a populace that wants consumer protection. Although there are national standards for utilities, each state has its own "watchdog" agency. There are national standards and some common needs regarding real estate, but the ultimate decision and "watchdog" status for real estate will remain local.

Swanepoel: There is no compelling reason that it will happen soon, but in principal I see no substantive reason why not to have federal licensing of real estate agents.

Question 14: Are the courts likely to overturn the various recent approaches to agency and say, in effect, that no agent and no firm can represent both a buyer and a seller at the same time under any circumstances?

Abelson: No. As people in the industry become more professional, we will see better handling of the dual agency issue. The risk of legislating against dual agency will therefore decrease over time. The risk of legislation against dual agency is currently minimal for another reason as well. There is not a large enough outcry for this type of legislation to overcompensate the increasingly intense national value against legislation that restricts or mandates the way businesses do business.

Swanepoel: I have no doubt that this issue will be in and out of the courts a few times during the next couple of years. No prediction on the decision of the courts in the United States is a safe one, and we will just have to wait and see.

Dooley: Place your money on the line and take whichever side of this bet makes you feel comfortable. My guess is that there are 50/50 odds either way. But, because of the litigiousness rampant in society, I would lay 80/20 odds that one or more such cases are actually brought to court.

Question 15: Has the percentage of home owner-ship in the United States reached its obtainable cap at about 65 percent or 66 percent?

Abelson: The percentage of home ownership seems to be relatively stagnant at this mid-60-percent level. I believe that the percentage of home ownership has potential of increasing, however, for two reasons. First, as Americans become more affluent, people will want and be better able to afford home ownership. Home ownership is a cultural value of both current Americans and those who are immigrating to the United States. Second, as the cities and existing homes age, the price of homes in numerous markets will remain relatively steady or decrease, allowing more people to be able to afford to purchase a home.

In order for the percentage of home ownership to increase, however, the current law allowing for the home interest payment deduction on federal income taxes will need to remain intact. If the deduction is taken away, the percentages of the population owning homes most likely will decrease.

Dooley: Just about. It may be able to nudge up a point or two, perhaps even cresting near 70 percent, if the federal government has any success in its programs to make home ownership available for lower income families.

Swanepoel: Tough call. I believe that the next generation of Americans will have a slightly lower desire to own their own homes and as such would suggest that the percentage will decline. However with the growing number of immigrants, and their strong pursuit of the "American dream," I would speculate that the numbers will balance out and on the whole remain fairly stable.

Question 16: Will ad valorem real estate taxes continue to be the major financing source for local governmental bodies and schools?

Dooley: *A* major, yes. *The* major, no—because governmental agencies will continue to scour the countryside searching for new things to tax and new ways to tax them. As more funding is raised for schools, there will be more insistence for greater options in the use of said funds (e.g., charter schools, magnet schools, parent vouchers, etc).

Swanepoel: Yes, I would expect so, although I am confident that the government will find additional funding sources should they need to.

Abelson: Yes. Even in the State of Texas, where there is a current movement regarding ad valorem taxes, the movement is toward decreasing the tax, not eliminating it. The State of Texas state legislatures, for example, with the governor's support, tried to develop a system that would allow for a dramatic decrease in the ad valorem tax. The outcome is a decrease on the reliance, but the reliance is still significant and remains a major source of revenue. The reliance on these taxes across the country will continue for the foreseeable future.

Question 17: Is the real estate appraising profession doomed and destined to be replaced by computerized statistical analysis?

Abelson: No. The appraisal industry is experiencing similar pressures as is the residential real estate industry. Technology is creating all types of dangers and opportunities. The appraisal industry may downsize in the number of appraisers needed because of the increased efficiencies. For the foreseeable future, however, there will remain the need for the human professional appraiser to oversee the process and make those decisions that are contributed to because of the uniqueness and changing qualities of each property.

Dooley: Not when it comes to rendering valuations for large-scale and top-dollar projects, but the "drive-by" estimate of the value of a residence is being replaced by a much more highly refined conjecture of value, based on computerized analyses of comparables and standard elements of worth.

Swanepoel: Yes, and they are but the first of a few functionalities and/or professions that might find themselves casualties of technology development. It is sad to see a profession almost completely disappear compared to what existed a decade or two ago. However, business calls it *progress,* and from the change in the appraising profession, numerous new opportunities have sprung up, creating new appraising-type business ventures.

Question 18: How will the standard profile of a real estate agent in the first decade of 2000 differ from the 1990s?

Swanepoel: The change for the current generation might seem gradual and maybe even insignificant. However, when we look back one day, we will probably note that the period from the end of the 1990s to the beginning of the 2000s was a period of significant change. The successful real estate agent of tomorrow will be more computer literate, probably younger and more knowledgeable about a broader base of real estate transaction-related issues, will be more focused on buyers than on sellers, will be on a salary plus commission structure and will be able to personally execute more components of the transaction in-house than his or her counterpart of today. In summary, the agent will change from selling to representing clients and facilitating transactions.

Abelson: We will see numerous dramatic shifts. Technology, consumer needs and demography (both increasing age and changes in race composition) will be the driving forces. A proportion of current agents will reach the age where they remove themselves from selling real estate. Increased reliance on technology, increased competition among agents, and increasing demands by consumers will make it difficult for these people to compete because they will have a difficult time adapting to the new demands. One profile will see younger, more flexible agents who have more formal education (college and graduate school training). Another profile will see a more culturally diverse real estate workforce. As demographics of age, race and sexual orientation change, so will the composition of the real estate agent profile. We will see agents creating market niches along these demographic lines depending on their own demographic makeup.

We will also see a continuation of the current real estate agent profile. This agent is typically white with some level of formal education above high school. Many agents will be second-career people, but more and more will enter the field so that early in their lives real estate is their first career.

Things that most agents will have in common are their willingness to use technology, willingness to change and their tremendous orientation toward customer service. If you don't have these three things, you won't be very successful in the business in the year 2000 and beyond.

Dooley: He or she will be much more career-oriented toward real estate. The field will be a primary rather than secondary source of income. There will be a higher percentage of men in residential sales than at present and a higher percentage of women in management and ownership than at present. Many will follow well-established corporate procedures in their daily operations rather than rely on individual "freelance" approaches to success.

Question 19: To what extent will real estate companies and real estate transactions be globalized by 2010?

Swanepoel: Globalization is a subject we deliberately decided not to address in the book as it is in its own a major trend in the coming decade. Having lived on three different continents, I can tell you that long before the year 2010 all of the major real estate companies will have offices on all the major continents. In many countries they will even be the dominant force. The advent of the Internet is making global expansion and communication even easier than before. Real estate data from around the world will, in the coming decade, be housed in a few global data warehouses and will be accessed from anywhere. Real estate will increasingly become a commodity, and international purchasing and ownership of real estate will become even more common-place than they already are today. Globalization together with technology has and will continue to open thousands of opportunities for shrewd businesses.

Abelson: Real estate transactions will become increasingly globalized as we approach the year 2010. This process, via the Internet, has already started and will continue to intensify. Prospective buyers are touring listings over the Internet. More people are even purchasing properties sight unseen. This is especially occurring for resort properties in certain areas of the United States. Expect to see it more often in other areas in the United States as well as in other countries.

We may even see more standardization of the real estate-transaction process across countries. The likelihood of this occurring however is limited to the extent the cultures of the people in those countries differ. In other words, some practices may be standardized across some countries, but don't expect an international standard process anytime soon, if ever.

Dooley: There will be a series of interlocking relationships among entities in various countries. Franchises will grow overseas in the form of master contracts with foreign nationals. However, it is doubtful if an individual firm or groups of firms will operate on a global scale, at least in the residential field. There is too much market to conquer at home.

Question 20: List and comment briefly on the three most significant changes or developments that will be apparent in the real estate brokerage industry by the period 2000 to 2005.

Abelson: (1) Demographics, (2) entry of a new player and accompanying paradigm shift and (3) a paradigm shift within the industry, where brokers are regaining control of the office by offering "value-added services" that agents are willing to purchase and excited about purchasing.

1.   The demography of the United States will have several significant impacts on the industry. There are eight different cohorts that are at different stages of home-buying and have different home-buying philosophies. As these cohorts move through the home-buying cycle, people in each cohort will significantly contribute in different ways to the industry (see Chapter 5 on consumer demographics). Also, immigration will have an overall neutral effect across all 50 states, but three states in particular (California, Texas and Florida) will see a significant cultural shift that will affect who buys and sells homes. Look for the makeup of the REALTOR® communities in these three states to change as well. Also, the baby boomers will continue to impact the industry. The next wave of impact of the baby boomer group will be second and vacation homes. Watch for the second and vacation home markets to grow significantly now and start to decrease about 2005 or thereafter.

2.   This change will see a new player who introduces a new technology or a new paradigm that significantly affects how things are done in the industry. This new player will make HFS's entry seem tame. Why? Because they will have a new, more efficient process for the real estate transaction that will threaten the way we do business. To prepare for this new entrant, it will be necessary to do everything in your power to increase the efficiency and effectiveness of the agent, the broker and the management of the brokerage business. This is not gloom and doom but a concern I believe we all need to prepare for.

3.   This trend has already begun. It is so extensive that it will take several years to have an effect. That effect will continue to build and increase in significance until at least the year 2005. We are currently seeing the broker implement systems that will enhance the effectiveness and efficiency of the office. These changes will be so significant that they will

be welcomed by agents and everyone else, especially the consumer. These new systems will be technology oriented and will streamline and speed the entire real estate-transaction process. These technology solutions will help with compensation/reward systems and unify the front office with the back office, with listing data and with people-management data. Agents will use these improvements because they add value to their job and allow them to interact more effectively and efficiently with their clientele. These systems will help prepare the industry to compete with the entry of an external paradigm shifter that, I predict, will enter the industry sometime between now and the year 2005.

Dooley: 1. The totality of the real estate transaction will be centralized, probably with the real estate firm in the center of activity, but centralized for sure.

2. Large firms will dominate the industry. There will be comparability to the retail food business. The "supermarkets" will command the vast bulk of the business. "Convenience" stores and "specialty" shops will still be around, but they will be quite peripheral to the major players. Also, the major firms will function much more smoothly across state lines because there will be universal reciprocity in recognizing licensing of real estate personnel.

3. The efforts of brokerage firms to generate more business through "pull" marketing activities controlled by the firm and less through "push" tactics controlled by the agents will bear substantial fruit. Results: (A) Greater share of company revenue retained by the brokerage and less by the agents, (B) more preferred vendor and affinity partner relationships and (C) probably some form of structuring of agents as employees rather than as independent contractors.

Swanepoel: If you do not stay ahead of the trends, everything you have worked for can and will be destroyed. It is strange. It would seem everyone generally likes progress, yet few really like change. Well, unfortunately, the future will not wait while you prepare for it. It's on course, its own of course, and will be arriving at the station whether you are there to greet it or not.

The three most significant trends for the next five years, I believe, are

1. the restructuring of the traditional MLS systems as we know them today and the increasing accessibility of real estate information by the consumer, anytime, anywhere and at nominal cost;

2. the increasing growth in the knowledge of the consumer, the new demands that this more-educated consumer will place on the real estate practitioner and the resulting growth of buyer agents to satisfy that phenomenon; and

3. the explosion of the Internet as a communication and marketing vehicle together with the significant role it will play in integrating the different components of the home-buying process into one easier, simpler process.

*I*NDEX

DR. MICHAEL ABELSON

Dr. Abelson is a full-time faculty member at Texas A&M University, has an active consulting practice, Abelson & Company, and delivers more than 50 speeches and seminars to real estate and other business audiences each year.

A former Research Fellow at the prestigious Center for Real Estate Research at Texas A&M, Abelson has completed 14 major studies of the real estate industry to date. Dr. Abelson has won numerous awards as an educator. He was recently listed in a special Business Week publication ranking outstanding teachers in leading MBA programs. His achievements have earned him recognition in *Who's Who in Science and Technology* and *Who's Who of Emerging Leaders in America*.

Specializing in leadership, effective change management and strategic thinking/planning, he is considered one of the leading authorities on the future of real estate. Dr. Abelson has published over 100 articles in *Fortune, Today's Realtor, The Washington Post* and every major real estate publication. His television shows, Abelson ProPerformer™ Show and Research Edge™ Report, have been featured on each of the three real estate TV networks.

Abelson & Company, founded in 1986, includes among its list of clients The Realty Alliance, GTE, the United States Army Corps of Engineers, PHH, Coldwell Banker, Century 21, RE/MAX and Compensation-Master.

Residing in College Station, Texas. He can be reached via e-mail at abelson@abelson-co.com.

THOMAS W. DOOLEY

Considered by many as the "Dean of Real Estate", Tom Dooley has been a well known and highly respected name in the real estate industry for nearly four decades.

In 1977 Mr. Dooley formed TWD & Associates, a consulting company that continues to serve the industry today. Clients include: HFS, Inc., ERA Franchise Systems, Inc., Coldwell Banker Real Estate, the National Association of REALTORS®, the Personal Marketing Company and US Digital.

In 1992 Mr. Dooley demonstrated his understanding of the real estate industry and its direction. He and partner Charles Dahlheimer acquired the then obscure Real Estate Buyer's Agent Council (REBAC). Today REBAC is part of NAR and is growing at a rate of 1,000 members per month.

Tom has authored numerous articles for such trade journals as: *Today's Realtor, Real Estate Today, The Real Estate Professional, Real Estate Review* and *National Relocation and Real Estate Magazine.* He is currently editor of *The Buyers Rep,* and *The Dooley/Dahlheimer Report: Real Estate In the 90s,* both monthly newsletters, and he has authored five books. Tom has also been a moderator and/or host on three different real estate television programs: "Great Ideas in Real Estate", "The Dooley/Dahlheimer Satellite Report" (both on RETN) and "Up Close and Personal" (on Realnet Direct).

Tom resides in Arlington Heights, Illinois, and can be reached via e-mail at Tdoo@aol.com.

STEFAN SWANEPOEL

Prior to relocating to the United States, Mr. Swanepoel almost single-handedly rewrote the rules in the South African real estate industry. Mr. Swanepoel is credited with having created the largest residential real estate brokerage in Africa, with 155 offices. Mr. Swanepoel launched the first U.S. real estate franchise, ERA, in Africa which he grew to 120 offices within two years.

Mr. Swanepoel served as Executive Vice President for the NAR equivalent in South Africa, and as Vice President of the nation's largest S&L where he participated with the acquisition of large real estate companies.

Mr. Swanepoel is most noted for conceptualizing and subsequently building in 1991 the first integrated multiple-listing and computerized-loan-application system in the world. This system is considered one of the best examples of real-estate transaction integration today.

Mr. Swanepoel served as Vice President for ERA in California in 1994/1995, and was promoted to Senior Vice President in 1996 when HFS purchased ERA. Stefan directed strategic development until January 1997, when he became president of US Digital Corporation.

Stefan was voted "Businessman of the Year" in 1987 and one of the "Ten Most Outstanding Young South Africans" in 1993. In 1996, *Today's Realtor* listed Stefan as one of the top "Movers and Shakers" in the U.S. real estate industry.

Stefan lives in Laguna Niguel, California. He can be reached via e-mail at Sswanepoel@aol.com or Sswanepoel@us-digital.com

ALMON R. BUD SMITH

Almon R. (Bud) Smith is Executive Vice President of the National Association of REALTORS®, the nation's largest trade association, representing nearly 800,000 members involved in all aspects of the real estate industry.

Smith, who officially assumed the Executive Vice President post in November 1991, has more than 25 years of experience within the National Association of REALTORS®. He has served as the executive officer of the Ohio Association of REALTORS®, the Cleveland Area Board of REALTORS® and the Cincinnati Board of REALTORS®.

Among his many NAR committee assignments, Smith served on the association's Board of Governors for the Executive Officers Seminar and was dean of the Seminar in 1976. He was a member of NAR's Executive Officers Committee from 1971 to 1988 and was the national chairman in 1979. He also served for two years on NAR's Executive Committee.